Hoover Institution Studies 39

Truman, the Jewish Vote, and the Creation of Israel

Truman, the Jewish Vote, and the Creation of Israel

John Snetsinger

Hoover Institution Press
Stanford University
Stanford, California

The Hoover Institution on War, Revolution and Peace, founded at Stanford University in 1919 by the late President Herbert Hoover, is a center for advanced study and research on public and international affairs in the twentieth century. The views expressed in its publications are entirely those of the authors and do not necessarily reflect the views of the staff, officers, or Board of Overseers of the Hoover Institution.

Hoover Institution Studies 39
International Standard Book Number 0–8179–3391–3
Library of Congress Card Number 70–187267
© 1974 by the Board of Trustees of the
     Leland Stanford Junior University

To the Memory of
Robert F. Kennedy

Contents

Preface

This book is a product of my interest in the formulation of United States foreign policy. The American role in the creation of Israel seemed an especially promising topic for inquiry because of the rich interplay of ideological issues and group interests that conditioned policy in this area. Probably the very richness of the topic accounts for the large quantity of sensational journalism dealing with Israel; the prevalent emotionalism makes a scholarly treatment all the more desirable. Because domestic pressures were so crucially involved in the decision-making process, this study is in large measure addressed to the domestic politics of the Truman administration. Foreign policy is never created in a vacuum, and I have tried to demonstrate here the vital link that exists between national politics and international relations.

Two generous grants enabled me to complete this book— one from the Harry S. Truman Institute for National and International Affairs, the other from California Polytechnic State University, San Luis Obispo. Basic research on the origin of American-Israeli relations must begin with an examination of the presidential papers of Harry Truman. While studying at the Truman Library in Independence, Missouri, I found the entire staff of the library both helpful and competent. The Truman Library also contains a significant collection of the papers of presidential adviser Clark Clifford. In addition, the White House papers on Palestine-Israel were consulted.

Throughout this project, and on many occasions while I was a graduate student at Stanford University, Professor Thomas A. Bailey assisted me with his great knowledge and experience. I am happy also to acknowledge the help of four other friends and colleagues at Stanford, Professor Barton J.

Bernstein, Steven Kotz, Lise Hofmann, and Professor George S. Rentz; they have been ungrudging and insightful. Everyone who has prepared a manuscript will understand my desire to thank Ms. J. Elise Snetsinger for help and patience without end. I hope this book shares some of their strengths, but such flaws as it contains result from my ignorance or obstinacy, or both.

Introduction

An extraordinary campaign aimed at influencing the direction of United States foreign policy was waged during the late 1940s. America's Jewish community, emotionally committed to assisting the European Jews who survived the Nazi genocide, attempted to secure the support of President Harry S. Truman's administration in behalf of establishing a Jewish state in Palestine. Initial presidential indecision was eventually replaced by Truman's active sponsorship of policies relating to the Jewish state that were desired by the overwhelming majority of Jews in America. Jewish leaders had indeed been persuasive; by the end of 1948 the State of Israel could rightly count on Truman as a good friend. This book is an account of the successful effort on the part of American Jews to win the president to the cause to which they were so deeply committed.

Only when the Second World War ended did Jews in this country learn of the full extent to which Hitler's policy of extermination had been fulfilled. As the stories of death trains, gas chambers, and mass graves continued to multiply, there emerged, quite naturally, a sense of responsibility among American Jews to assist the small remnant of European Jewry who had escaped only to find themselves languishing in displaced persons camps. Few of the remaining one million Jewish refugees wished to return to their European nation of origin. It was widely believed among the survivors that their future safety could be guaranteed only once they were within an autonomous Jewish state. American Jews responded to the plight of these refugees in several ways. Supplies, money, and volunteer assistance were rushed to Europe. These contributions, however, ensured only immediate relief.

For the dream of a Jewish state in Palestine to become a reality, it was generally thought that the government of the United States would have to play a positive diplomatic role on its behalf. Within the American Jewish community, it became an issue of the highest priority to convince the president to use this country's influence to transfer the refugees to Palestine and then to sponsor the establishment of a Jewish state there. It is not difficult to understand why so many Jews in the United States worked to shape the direction of this specific aspect of foreign policy. The reasons for their vigorous campaign stem from the experiences of their fellow Jews in Europe during the war. Since many of the Jewish displaced persons viewed the issue of creating their own state as being nothing less than a matter of survival, Jews in the United States approached their task with a firm commitment to succeed.

Ethnic minorities in the United States have often been able to apply pressure and shape a specific area of diplomatic policy that interests them. Although this book is concerned solely with relating the history of the successful efforts to influence the Truman administration's Palestine-Israel policy from 1945 to 1948, the events of those years do not represent an isolated case in this nation's history. Other ethnic minorities have attempted to influence foreign policy, although in recent years none have approached the Jewish achievement.

All forms of government, including dictatorships, ultimately rely upon the support of public opinion to sustain their activities abroad. In a democracy the link between the nation's diplomacy and the desires of the citizenry is more direct than in nondemocratic states. Despite the increasingly unpopular Vietnam involvement, the author's reading of the historical record leads him to accept the view that the American electorate generally does determine the basic outlines of its government's foreign policy.

For example, one cause of the Spanish-American War in 1898 was the bellicose reaction of the American public to the events of that year. Even though President William McKinley was personally opposed to the conflict, his opposition to it weakened when the public called for war after the battleship *Maine* exploded and sank to the bottom of the Havana harbor. John Adams, in a similar situation, refused to yield to popular pressure for war with France in 1800 although he sensed the political consequences. Disgruntled citizens have used their electoral power to remove officeholders whose diplomatic postures were at odds with the popular mood. The president, as the leader of a major political party, may have such a commitment to his political allies that he will not conduct a foreign policy that might endanger the party's chances of future success.[1]

Astute politicians must not only be aware of broad-based national sentiment concerning a diplomatic issue, but must also give a hearing to ethnic minorities who have a particular interest in certain areas of the country's foreign policy. Millions of immigrants to the United States retained previous national or religious loyalties. Organized ethnic minorities can bring pressure on the government for specific policies which are peculiarly their own and which may favor their original homeland vis-à-vis another nation, or a particular political movement within that country, or simply reflect an attitude which is common to similar American immigrant groups.

The extent to which ethnic minorities are able to shape foreign policy is a uniquely American phenomenon. No other nation absorbed such extensive waves of immigration as did the United States. Sixty percent of the world's international migration between the early nineteenth century and 1930 came to America. An indication of the result of this migration is the fact that in 1950 approximately 34 million out of the total population of 150 million were either immigrants themselves or had at least one immigrant parent.[2]

So apparent and consistent are the desired diplomatic policies of some ethnic minorities that politicians can frequently anticipate what actions will solidify support for themselves among these groups. Even though the resulting positions may flout foreign policy objectives outlined by Washington, these politicians have made attempts to please the large ethnic blocs within their constituency. Mayor "Big Bill" Thompson, for example, placated those citizens of Irish extraction when he pledged he would "punch the snout" of the King of England should the monarch dare to enter Chicago. More recently New York City's Mayor Robert Wagner, pursuing a policy that was designed to meet with the approval of his city's three million Jews, refused to welcome the Saudi Arabian ruler during a widely publicized goodwill tour of the United States.[3]

City mayors and other local officials may irritate foreign leaders, but the extent to which such actions affect American diplomacy is relatively slight. More serious consequences can arise when ethnic minorities place sufficient pressures on the national government to alter the direction of foreign policy. Since 1900, for example, the development of a close understanding between the United States and Great Britain has been blocked on several occasions by persistent anglophobia that centered among those citizens of Irish and German ancestry. These two minorities opposed early American intervention to aid Britain in both world wars. Due in part to such opposition, Washington not only postponed early wartime alliances with Britain, but peacetime rapprochement also was handled in every instance with extreme caution.[4]

Ethnic groups are not based only on national origin, but may instead be formed on the basis of a religious attachment. Jews, for example, represent one of the most forceful ethnic blocks in the United States today. Prior to the twentieth century relatively few Jews lived in the United States. Only during the early 1900s did Jews emerge as a prominent minority within the nation. In 1902 anti-Semitic persecutions in Rumania resulted in American Jews requesting United States intervention. Secretary of State John Hay, although he privately believed it to be an internal Rumanian question, issued a stern protest to the Rumanian government. Sent in part to assist the

Republicans in the approaching 1902 election, the protest apparently constituted a politically successful move for the party.[5] Organized Jewish interest in American foreign affairs since the early years of the century has largely focused on attempts to secure substantive support for the establishment of a Jewish state in Palestine. The history of that effort in the period following World War II will be traced in this book.

A final point should be made concerning the impact of ethnic minorities upon American foreign policy. Most immigrants to America sought to become loyal citizens of their adopted country, but a complete adjustment was blocked by the American society itself. Immigrants, relegated to ghettos formed on national or religious bases, had to seek a renewed association with the causes of their foreign brethren in order to bolster their self-esteem. Political parties and opportunistic politicians have consistently, and in a potentially damaging manner, encouraged ethnic voters to cast their ballots on the basis of ancestral ties. Promises to assist various foreign causes are carelessly pledged by candidates. Much of the politicking that takes place is unfortunate, for it is often not in the best interest of an intelligent foreign policy to be subject to the influences of domestic politics.[6]

Organizing for a Jewish State

THE DEVELOPMENT OF ZIONISM

Palestine was the locale of a Jewish state that had existed for hundreds of years. In the first century A.D., the Hebrew people revolted against the Romans who indirectly ruled Judea. Jewish life in Palestine declined rapidly after a series of unsuccessful rebellions. Although other movements advocating the reestablishment of a Jewish state existed prior to modern times, the Zionist crusade was initiated during the 1890s. Early in the decade an epidemic of virulent anti-Semitism swept across Europe. A young Austrian Jew, Theodor Herzl, suggested that the solution to anti-Semitism could be found in the establishment of a modern national home for Jews.

Zionism, the modern Hebrew movement calling for creation of a Jewish homeland, was politically structured by the 1897 congress summoned by Herzl and his supporters. Although the congress initially endorsed a vague resolution favoring only a "home in Palestine," it was not long before the central Zionist policy was the establishment of a Jewish state in Palestine. The 1897 congress created the World Zionist Organization, which remained the official voice of world Zionism. Chaim Weizmann assumed the leadership of the movement after Herzl's death in 1904. Herzl and Weizmann both rejected assimilation of the Jew as a solution to his difficulties; only by establishing their own state could Jews overcome the chilling consequences of anti-Semitism.[1]

World War I placed the Zionists in a favorable bargaining position. Great Britain was anxious to generate more enthusiastic support among the world's Jews for the Allied cause. An official pro-Zionist statement offered the British an opportunity to arouse some flagging Jewish interest.[2] The British were concerned, however, that any statement favoring Jewish aims in the Middle East would endanger the friendships that had recently been developed with the Arab leadership. Britain was particularly hesitant to announce any pro-Zionist pledge without official support from its American ally. A "declaration of sympathy" with Zionism by President Woodrow Wilson would dispel the British concern of becoming diplomatically isolated on the Palestine issue. The president's response was negative, however, when the British informally broached the subject with Wilson in early September, 1917. Wilson, with the advice of Colonel Edward House, expressed the opinion that "the time was not opportune" for such a statement. Any hope that the Ottoman Empire might be persuaded to drop out of the war could be shattered by an Allied announcement that dealt with the future disposition of land within the Empire's boundaries. Firm opposition toward any pro-Zionist pledge was also advised by Secretary of State Robert Lansing and the State Department.[3]

Led by their most influential American spokesman, Louis Brandeis, the Zionists made a concerted effort to reverse Wilson's decision. As chairman of the Provisional Committee for General Zionist Affairs from 1914 to 1916, Brandeis became the acknowledged Zionist leader in America by drawing together all divergent factions of the movement. Brandeis, at the time a justice of the United States Supreme Court as well as an esteemed unofficial adviser to Wilson, has been credited with changing the president's mind. The jurist's persuasive power was used first to convince House and then to bring Wilson himself over to the Zionist side. Wilson and House dropped their misgivings after meeting individually with Brandeis on September 23, 1917.[4]

When a few weeks later the British again asked Wilson for his views concerning the proposed declaration on a Jewish homeland, the president answered that he now favored a British statement. Wilson's first response had come close to forestalling any British announcement. Had the president's reply to the second inquiry been similar to the first, it is quite possible that the British would not have issued a statement on Zionism.[5] The Zionists, by their ability to swing Wilson from disapproval to endorsement through direct personal intervention, set a precedent that would be used later with even more striking results during the Truman administration.

In November 1917 the Zionists attained their signal victory. Great Britain's foreign secretary, Arthur Balfour, in a letter to Lord Rothschild, declared:

> His Majesty's Government views with favor the establishment in Palestine of a national home for the Jewish people, and will use their best endeavours to facilitate the achievement of this objective, it being clearly understood that nothing shall be done which may prejudice the civil and religious rights of existing non-Jewish communities in Palestine, or the rights and political status enjoyed by Jews in any other country.[6]

It is difficult to discern the extent of Britain's responsibility as a result of Balfour's words. The declaration was imprecise; but neither the Zionists nor the British were anxious at the time to probe the exact meaning of the language. London did not give an assurance that the government would be directly responsible for a Jewish state. Great Britain agreed only to use its "best endeavours" in order to "facilitate" the establishment of a Jewish "national home." All key words in this political, not legal, document were, according to historian Leonard Stein's analysis, "studiously vague." [7] Britain did, however, at least make a commitment to give moral support for the creation of a Jewish homeland in Palestine.

In 1920 the triumphant Allies compelled Turkey, who had ruled Palestine since 1517, to cede the territory to the victors. The Allies then entrusted sovereign jurisdiction for Palestine to the League of Nations. Britain, anxious to extend her influence in the Middle East and protect her access to India, received in turn a mandate to administer Palestine from the League. Although the League of Nations grant instructed Great Britain to carry out the pledges made in the Balfour Declaration, London moved to discourage the formation of a Jewish homeland.[8] In 1939 a British white paper served as the basis for a policy which contributed to the tragedy of the European Jews in subsequent years. The document recommended a policy of drastic limitation, and eventual termination, of the flow of Jewish immigrants into Palestine. Under the terms of the mandate, Great Britain had agreed to keep the gates of Palestine open to Jews. The League of Nations was on the verge of revoking the Palestine mandate as a result of British violations when the Second World War began.[9]

Implementation of Nazi Germany's "final solution" to the so-called Jewish problem during the war resulted in the deaths of six million Jews. Most Jewish survivors of the Nazi terror in Europe were convinced of the Zionist vew that there would be no safety until the Jews were rooted in a nation of their own. More than ever before, Zionists were convinced that their program provided Jews with the one feasible alternative to future pogroms. Zionists also realized that if they were ever to secure a state, the immediate postwar period would provide the most propitious time. A wave of sympathy existed for the Jews in 1945; it was expected that this support could prove to be an aid in trying to implement the Zionist program.[10]

ZIONISM IN THE UNITED STATES

In the United States the Zionists emerged from the war in a powerful position within the Jewish community. American

Jewry was stunned by the Hitler nightmare, and the vast majority either joined Zionist organizations or solidly supported their program as a means of ensuring against a similar ordeal in the future. A poll taken by Elmo Roper in 1945 indicated that only one Jew in ten was against establishing a Jewish state in Palestine.[11] By 1948 an impressive total of 711,000 Jews had joined Zionist organizations. These groups engaged in a variety of charitable and social activities aside from working for the fulfillment of Zionism's political goals. Over a half million persons belonged to the affiliate of the World Zionist Organization, the Zionist Organization of America.[12]

Two skillful leaders, Stephen Wise and Abba Hillel Silver, assumed co-chairmanship positions of the American Zionist Emergency Council (AZEC) in 1943. This council, which was a representative body comprising all American Zionist groups, launched an aggressive and centralized political offensive and coordinated all official Zionist public relations in the United States. Almost immediately the American Zionist Emergency Council was transformed into a model of organizational competence. The council's workload was smoothly handled by its fourteen professionally staffed committees. In addition, more than 400 local American Zionist Emergency committees were formed in an effort to extend the public relations campaign to both Jews and non-Jews in all important American communities. The local committees were urged to keep political officeholders and community leaders informed of the aims and objectives of AZEC. The sound financial position of AZEC, with an average annual budget in excess of $500,000, enabled it to perform with such efficiency.[13]

The organizational strength developed by the Zionists was strikingly displayed in the White House-directed mail campaigns. Adopting a tactic frequently used by successful pressure groups, the project was enthusiastically supported by sympathetic citizens. Personal letters, postcards, telegrams, resolutions, and form letters on the Palestine issue were dispatched to the president. An accurate count of the mail received is not available, but when White House aides undertook an analysis of the Palestine mail in 1951, over one million pieces were still in storage. For one three-month period during 1948, 301,900 postcards were found in a White House depository. Nearly all of the mail received on the Palestine issue came from Jewish interest groups and their supporters. Most of the correspondence urged that Truman support an immediate objective sought by the Zionists whereas only a small percentage appealed directly to the president to champion the overall campaign for a Jewish state.[14]

The conspicuous number of form letters the White House received indicated the careful direction the leadership gave to the mail campaigns. Organizations asked for participation in their mail campaigns and suggested the contents of the letters. Rather than rewrite the proffered message, as the mimeographed or dittoed directions stipulated, some persons merely signed the instruction sheets and mailed them to Wahington.[15] All elements within the Jewish community were asked to write. One handbill urged pupils in Jewish schools to

> send a letter to the President of the United States, or a postcard, similar to the following. Re-write it in your own words. "I am a student in the___(name)___Hebrew School in ___(place)___. I am_____years of age. Please help the Jewish boys and girls in Palestine so that they can win their battle for freedom." [16]

American Jews were willing to respond to the cause by contributing considerably more than letters. Zionist officials in Palestine recognized that it would take a massive infusion of both money and supplies to realize the hope of a viable Jewish state. The fight for national independence relied in part on sympathizers abroad. When the Jewish Agency for Palestine, the official spokesman for Jews in Palestine,[17] requested financial and material support during the pre-Israel years of 1945–48, the response from American Jews was notably positive. An example of such generosity occurred when Golda Meir spoke of the immediate need for cash during a 1948 fund-raising campaign organized by the Jewish Agency. Within a matter of days Mrs. Meir received pledges for twenty-five million dollars.

Among the most dependable sponsors the Agency had in this country was an organization of a select group of Jewish businessmen euphemistically called the Sonneborn Institute, after its founder, Rudolf Sonneborn. These men raised the money and purchased many millions of dollars' worth of supplies needed by the Jewish Agency to launch the new state. The extent of the Institute's financial commitment was tested at a regular meeting in late 1947 when a Jewish Agency representative informed the seventy-two members present that five million dollars would have to be raised in two weeks. Convinced that a Jewish state might not have a chance of surviving without their help, the Institute's membership collected the money within the time limit. During 1948 the Sonneborn Institute funneled more than a million dollars a month of noncontraband supplies into Palestine. In addition to noncontraband supplies, the Institute attempted to provide a wide variety of illegal goods.[18]

It was essential to the Jews in Palestine that they have military equipment to defend themselves once the new state came into being. Fortunately for the Jewish Agency, the United States had instructed its War Assets Administration to auction off much of its wartime arsenal; exceptional bargains were available for buyers as a result. On one occasion the American who was surreptitiously buying for the Jewish Agency managed to purchase machinery used for weapons production that had originally cost approximately a quarter of a million dollars for only $10,000. Surplus ships were bought for a small fraction of their original cost and used to transport Jewish immigrants to Palestine from the displaced persons camps in Europe. There were virtually no limits on the kind of materiel that was designated surplus and offered for sale. For ex-

ample, the Sonneborn Institute successfully bid on a 500-foot
aircraft carrier, *Attu,* for the bargain price of $125,000. The
Attu was broken up and sold for scrap when it became clear
that even the most artful deception would not make possible
its illegal delivery to the Jewish Agency.[19]

There was nothing illegal about purchasing millions of dollars' worth of war equipment from the United States government. It was assumed that buyers would either adapt the machinery to peacetime purposes or use it for scrap. Legal
problems emerged with the attempt to transport the goods to
Palestine. Washington opposed any wholesale shipment of sur-
plus weaponry to the growing Jewish army in the Middle
East. Friends of the Jewish Agency in America concluded
that the State Department would attempt to block all efforts
to arm the Jews because such action would frustrate the desire
of the British to keep Palestine tranquil until their withdrawal.
Since the legal transfer of military supplies was denied, a sophisticated underground endeavored to slip equipment out of
the country. Membership in the underground consisted largely
of American Jews who were deeply committed to the formation of a Jewish state. Despite federal and local restrictions,
the underground managed to deliver a high percentage of its
contraband. Vague front corporations, such as the Machinery
Processing and Converting Company, sent illegal cargoes,
falsely labeled "used industrial machinery," to the Jews in Palestine. Techniques of deception were employed to protect the
individuals involved from being traced. When a dockside load-
ing accident exposed a shipment of TNT, the layers of protec-
tive fronts were so effective that an exasperated Federal Bureau of Investigation was unable to discover which persons
were responsible for the illicit shipment.[20]

A particularly dramatic contribution made by the American underground was the establishment and operation of a
complete air base inside a Communist nation in 1948. At the
same time the United States and the Soviet Union were em-
broiled in a Cold War confrontation over Berlin, a largely

American contingent in Czechoslovakia was engaged in air-lifting to Palestine eighty-two planes that the Jewish Agency had purchased from the Czechoslovak government. Possession of the planes was an important factor in Israel's defense when the Arab armies attacked.[21]

Most of the Americans involved in assisting the Jewish Agency have not been interested in making known the nature of their contribution. The entire underground vanished as soon as Israel gave evidence that the continuation of such activities was no longer necessary. By systematically destroying records, organizations formed to assist the Jewish Agency were able to secure at least a degree of permanent anonymity. It is not therefore possible to trace accurately the extent of this financial and material aid. Those who contributed did so not for recognition but because they believed in the cause they aided.[22]

Another factor which favored the Zionists was the limited opposition to their aims on the part of the American public. Among Jews, for example, only a small percentage failed to support Zionism. The one anti-Zionist organization, the American Council for Judaism, never attained the level of support that critics of Zionism at the time had claimed for it. At its peak this council had only a few thousand members.[23] Also, the Zionists were virtually unchallenged by any other ethnic pressure group in American politics. Political parties did not worry about alienating an Arab vote since there was no significant Arab population in America.[24] Finally, the Zionist cause was aided by an American public that was either mildly sympathetic or at least apathetic. Three out of four persons with an opinion supported the Zionist demand that Palestine be opened to the large-scale immigration of Jewish refugees. The basic Zionist aim of establishing a Jewish state was consistently favored by those in the sample with an opinion, although at times the margin of support was as narrow as a few percentage points.[25]

Perhaps as significant as the opinions expressed was the fact that so large a percentage of the public did not follow the Palestine controversies. Only 45 percent of those questioned in one poll could identify Britain as the country that had the mandate for Palestine. As late as the fall of 1946, 49 percent admitted that they had not followed the discussion about establishing a Jewish national home.[26] Outside the Jewish community the Zionist program clearly did not raise very intense political issues.

2

Truman Seeks a Policy

CAUTION RECOMMENDED TO PRESIDENT

When Zionist dreams of establishing a Jewish state were fulfilled in 1948, the new nation honored Chaim Weizmann, for decades the recognized leader of the Zionist movement, by electing him the first president of Israel. A humble man, he minimized his own role and insisted that the person most responsible for giving birth to the first Jewish state in two thousand years was Harry S. Truman, the thirty-third president of the United States.[1] There is reason to believe that Weizmann, perhaps desiring to flatter the American chief executive, exaggerated the role Truman played in the creation of Israel. Yet the statement does attest to the substantial support Truman gave to the movement for a Jewish state. What is especially intriguing about Weizmann's analysis of the White House contribution is that it was unclear until 1948 whether the power of the American presidency was going to be used to aid or frustrate Zionist aspirations.

President Truman found himself torn between two conflicting camps within his administration, with both factions proposing alternate directions for Palestine policy. For three years a virtual tug-of-war existed between the State Department and its allies, on the one hand, and members of the president's personal staff on the other. During 1948 the latter emerged triumphant. In an election year influential aides convinced Truman of the political necessity of catering to American Jews by supporting the cause of Israel.

11

Only 5,600,000 Jews lived in the United States in the late 1940s, but they were so situated that their political influence far exceeded their numerical strength. Political strategists were aware that 65 percent of these American Jews were settled in three pivotal states—New York, Pennsylvania, and Illinois. With a total of 110 electoral votes at stake, these states provided attractive targets during the 1948 presidential campaign. Democratic party tacticians believed that significant numbers of Jews would withhold their votes from Truman if he failed to accommodate Jewish aspirations in the Middle East; a national election might thus be decided by a group of Jews displeased with the president's Palestine policy. Because there was virtually no voter opposition to the Jewish demands, presidential aides argued that Truman had everything to gain and nothing to lose by adopting friendly policies toward the establishment of a Jewish state.

By the time Truman became president, the battle lines in Washington were already drawn between adherents of a Palestine policy that catered to the Arabs and others who insisted upon decisions backing Jewish claims in the Middle East. Elements within the national government argued that it was reckless to risk America's strategic and economic interests in the postwar world by siding with Jew instead of Arab in the Middle East. Governmental opposition to Jewish plans for Palestine emanated from the State Department, the newly structured Department of Defense, and high-level military consultants.

Clearly the overriding American interest in the area was oil. As far back as the 1920s American oil companies began securing rights allowing them to share in the exploitation of the region's oil deposits. It was during World War II, however, that United States involvement in Arab oil reached a significant level. American engineers and economic experts, as well as troops, poured into the Middle East, all giving visible evidence of an expanding American interest in the petroleum resources.[2] Representing the greatest concentration of oil on earth, the Middle East contained two-thirds of the world's proved reserves in the late 1940s. The region's petroleum supply is easily accessible, of a high quality, and inexpensive to secure.[3]

Some government officials, including Secretary of Defense James Forrestal, warned in the late 1940s that America must insure for herself a continuing access to Middle Eastern oil. Forrestal argued that domestic production could not satisfy the nation's future requirements.[4] On the basis of most recent data, it appears that Forrestal was correct. It is currently estimated that United States reserves have a life span of twelve years. James Akins, director of the State Department's Office of Fuels and Energy, predicted on July 17, 1971, that "all projections" indicate an increased United States dependence on Arab petroleum.[5]

Strategists who gauged an eventual American requirement also accurately envisioned a crucial link between Western Europe's economic strength and its ability to secure fuel from the Middle East. The oil-poor European democracies rapidly increased their demand for Arab petroleum; postwar Europe was soon importing between 70 and 80 percent of the oil it used from Arab sources. Energy specialist Akins informed a congressional hearing, during his 1971 testimony, that American allies in Europe "are and will remain almost totally dependent" on Arab oil for the "foreseeable future." [6] Even before the Marshall Plan was proposed in early 1947, it was clear that the Truman administration considered the economic viability of Europe's democracies essential to Western security. Accordingly, European oil problems were also American problems. State Department and Defense Department tacticians wanted to avoid alienating those who controlled the flow of oil out of the Middle East. Hostile Arabs could make Western Europe's vulnerability a concern for the entire Western bloc.[7]

American economic interest in the area had increased at an astonishing rate. By early 1948 over 11,000 Americans were in the Arab lands, directing an investment of several hundred million dollars. One pipeline linking the oil pools of Saudi Arabia with the Mediterranean coast was being constructed by four American oil firms at a reported cost of 150 million dollars. Arab leaders expected to be able to use America's growing involvement in the Arab world to their advantage. By threatening to employ economic sanctions against United States oil interests, these Arabs sought to undercut Jewish efforts to secure American support for Zionist programs.[8] Civilian and military advisers within the Washington government were distressed by such threats. To these supporters of a pro-Arab policy, the most desirable condition for the Middle East was a perpetual peace which permitted coursing pipelines to furnish the anti-Communist world with a seemingly limitless quantity of "black gold." Zionism endangered this possibility with its aim of thrusting a Jewish state into the Middle Eastern political scene.[9]

Government advisers also valued American influence in the Arab world for reasons apart from the interest in oil. State Department and both civilian and military personnel in the Department of Defense viewed the area as a critically situated region that should not be allowed to ally itself with the Communist world. Located between two oceans and three continents, the Middle East was visualized as providing the Western powers with a base for establishing an extensive sea and air capacity directed against the Soviet Union.[10] It was also believed that any power vacuum which might result in Soviet hegemony in the region should be viewed as a potential catastrophe. Not only would Moscow "have its grip on Europe's jugular vein" by controlling the supply of oil, but Russian military dominance in the area was seen as possibly upsetting the balance of power in the world.[11] Spokesmen for the State Department, the Department of Defense, and the military agreed that the United States should adopt friendly policies toward the Arab nations and thereby insure that the region would maintain, and even strengthen, its bonds with the West.

Any program that weakened American-Arab friendship, as Zionist designs for a Jewish state threatened to do, was regarded as a menace to the national security of the United States.

TRUMAN'S INITIAL CONTACT WITH ZIONISM

While serving as a United States senator from 1935 to 1945, Truman had compiled a mixed record on the question of establishing a Jewish state in Palestine. He had publicly expressed his approval of the Zionist goal along with the majority of congressmen. In 1939, for example, Senator Truman inserted a newspaper article into the *Congressional Record* which strongly supported Zionist goals.[12] During World War II he sharply reduced his commitment when he decided that America's national interest would not be served by forcing the issue. The crusade for a national home, Truman believed, should wait until the more important problem of winning the war was resolved. In a letter to Stephen Wise, Truman bitterly withdrew his support from the Committee for a Jewish Army, deciding that one of their newspaper advertisements was "used to stir up trouble where our troops are fighting." According to Truman, the *New York Times* advertisement "was used by all the Arabs in North Africa in an endeavor to create dissension among them and caused them to stab our fellows in the back." "We want to help the Jews," Truman wrote, but ". . . we cannot do it at the expense of our military maneuvers."[13] A year later Truman cited the many diplomatic difficulties facing the Western powers, saying he did not "want to throw any bricks to upset the applecart at this time." Creating a Jewish state, the senator continued, was not an issue of the first priority, "although *when the right time comes* I am willing to help make the fight for a Jewish Home in Palestine."[14] The first official contact the new president had with the Palestine question occurred a few days after he took office, when Secretary of State Edward Stettinius sent Truman a letter that briefed him on the controversy. Stettinius said that Zionist leaders would soon try to secure Truman's commitment for their program of unlimited Jewish immigration into Palestine and the creation of a Jewish state. Presenting what was the standard State Department view, Stettinius suggested caution and reminded Truman that American interests in the Middle East were not to be lightly regarded. A few weeks later Truman's position was further complicated when he learned of his predecessor's ambivalent attitude in connection with Palestine.[15] Roosevelt had publicly praised the Zionists and endorsed their aim of establishing a Jewish state; [16] yet he also assured the Arab leaders that there would be no change in the basic situation in Palestine "without full consultation with Jews and Arabs." [17]

Joseph C. Grew, the acting secretary of state in Stettinius's absence, informed Truman that the State Department position was that the time was not propitious to raise the Palestine question since the war was not yet over. Grew felt that Palestine should be one of the issues handled by the United Nations once the war ended. He urged caution and asked Truman to refrain from making any commitments, especially to the Zionists.[18]

Truman accepted the State Department advice in the initial months of his administration. He approved a letter drafted by the State Department, similar to the ones Roosevelt had agreed to, assuring an Arab leader that "no decision should be taken respecting the basic situation in Palestine without full consultation with both Arabs and Jews." [19] During the summer of 1945, however, he began to question the department's ability to appreciate the humanitarian implications of its policy. Although Truman believed that some in the State Department sided with the Arabs for strategic and economic reasons, he added that he was "sorry to say that there were some among them who were also inclined to be anti-Semitic." [20] Truman was concerned about the plight of the Jewish refugees in Europe who wanted to start a new life. In the course of a press conference in August, he stated that American policy was "to let as many of the Jews into Palestine as it is possible to let into that country." [21] The president was apparently moved by a report he received from Earl G. Harrison late in August 1945. Truman had dispatched Harrison, dean of the University of Pennsylvania Law School, on a European mission to investigate the problems of displaced persons.[22] Harrison reported that the one million Jewish survivors still living in temporary refugee camps throughout Europe were behind barbed-wire fences in what had been concentration camps, and they survived on a diet consisting of bread and coffee. Most Jews hoped for a new beginning; they did not want to return to their country of origin. Harrison concluded his study by recommending that the "only real solution" would be the immediate evacuation to Palestine of those Jews who desired to leave Europe. However, complicating this solution to the refugee problem was Britain's policy, as stated in a 1939 white paper, that limited Jewish entry into Palestine by issuing 75,000 immigration certificates to the Jews. When the certificates were exhausted, no more were to be issued. Harrison was concerned that all immigration would cease because only a few scattered certificates were still outstanding. He wrote that it would be calamitous if the British were to keep Palestine closed to the Jews. The Zionists had proposed a plan whereby Great Britain would make available 100,000 additional certificates, and Harrison urged Truman to support this request.[23]

The State Department reacted by recommending to Truman that he refrain from supporting large-scale immigration; any policy that could offend the Arabs was to be avoided. Truman, however, was increasingly less inclined to accept such departmental advice on Jewish immigration. The State Department, Truman later wrote, was "more concerned about the Arab reaction than the sufferings of the Jews." [24]

Finding the Harrison report more convincing than State

Department entreaties to the contrary, Truman decided to seek a change in British policy. He wrote to Clement Attlee on August 31, 1945, and vigorously appealed to Britain's prime minister to accept the Zionist proposal and consent to the immediate immigration of 100,000 Jewish refugees into Palestine.[25] Directly challenging London's intention to shut the gates of Palestine, Truman told Attlee that Americans "firmly believe that immigration into Palestine should not be closed. . . ." Using language strikingly similar to Harrison's, the president suggested that the "main solution appears to lie in the quick evacuation of as many as possible of the non-repatriable Jews who wish it, to Palestine." [26]

Although Truman had ignored State Department suggestions by endorsing the liberal immigration schedule, Zionists expressed a growing dissatisfaction with the president. Jewish leaders wanted full administration support for their long-range goals; in particular they sought presidential support for creating a Jewish state.[27] Also, when Britain's first response to Truman's appeal of August 31 was to increase the campaign against Jews illegally entering Palestine, the Zionists were convinced the president was not doing all he could to influence the Attlee government. Rabbi Abba Hillel Silver mirrored the dismay and uncertainty that Zionists shared when he wrote, "What our Government intends to do in the Palestine matter is still a mystery to us." [28]

By the autumn of 1945 Truman's dilemma was one that was to occur again—his Palestine policy failed to please anyone. According to reports in the *New York Times,* British displeasure was aroused by the president's demand for increased Palestine immigration, and many Jews were convinced that Truman had no genuine commitment to the Zionist program. As far as the Arabs were concerned, American support of Jewish immigration was a hostile act.[29] "The Jewish and Arab situation," Truman wrote in October, ". . . has caused us more difficulty than most any other problem in the European Theater." [30]

The president's stature among Zionists was further damaged when Roosevelt's promises to the Arab leaders were revealed and Truman was forced to equivocate in respect to his Zionist commitments. The difficulty began when an Arab spokesman claimed that President Roosevelt had promised King ibn-Saud of Saudi Arabia that "he would not support the Jews in Palestine." [31] When asked at a press conference if the charge were valid, Truman responded by saying that there was no record of Roosevelt making any commitment to the king of Saudi Arabia.[32] Roosevelt never specifically promised he would not support the Zionist program, which was the claim of the Arab spokesman. Truman was apparently unaware, however, that Roosevelt had made any type of pledge to King ibn-Saud. The White House decided publicly to correct the president's error, according to Clifton Daniel, the *New York Times* correspondent in the Middle East, only after the king threatened to release the exchange of letters between himself and Roosevelt.[33]

On October 18, 1945, James Byrnes, the new secretary of state, was authorized by Truman to release the correspondence.[34] In his letter to ibn-Saud, written on April 5, 1945, in response to a March 10 letter from the king, Roosevelt reminded him that during their recent conversation, held in February 1945, "I assured you that I would take no action . . . which might prove hostile to the Arab people." Roosevelt, in recalling the "memorable" discussion, also remarked that he had obtained a "vivid . . . impression of Your Majesty's sentiments on this question" of Zionism.[35] It is likely that Roosevelt gave his letter, which he signed just a week before his death, only the most cursory review. Since the tone and language of the message suggest that it was a courtesy letter prepared by the State Department, it is possible that Roosevelt was not aware that any controversy could emerge out of the wording of the note.

Incredulity prevailed among Zionists even though Roosevelt had not personally spoken out in favor of the Zionist plans for Palestine. During the 1944 presidential campaign, however, Roosevelt authorized the AZEC co-chairman Stephen Wise to announce to the press that the Palestine plank in the Democratic party platform had the full backing of the president. The Democratic platform, in which the party pledged to support the Zionist program for both unlimited immigration and statehood, read: "We favor the opening of Palestine to unrestricted Jewish immigration and colonization, and such a policy is to result in the establishment there of a free and democratic Jewish commonwealth." [36] Just three weeks before the election, Roosevelt sent a message to members attending the Annual Conference of the Zionist Organization of America. In his statement, which was presented by Senator Robert Wagner of New York, the president was sympathetic. "I know how long and ardently the Jewish people have worked and prayed for the establishment of Palestine as a free and democratic Jewish commonwealth. I am convinced," Roosevelt said, "that the American people give their support to this aim and if re-elected I shall help to bring about its realization." Roosevelt promised that efforts would be made to find "appropriate ways and means of effectuating this policy as soon as possible." [37] The president's endorsement of his party's pledge to work in behalf of "a free and democratic Jewish commonwealth" simply did not square with his pledge to ibn-Saud that he "would take no action . . . which might prove hostile to the Arab people," for Arab leaders were committed to the establishment of an independent Arab state throughout all of Palestine.

Following his February 1945 private session with ibn-Saud, Roosevelt had written to Stephen Wise to assure him that he would work toward making the Zionist program a reality. Once Arab leaders announced that Roosevelt had made a commitment to them, the American Zionist Emergency Council released the president's letter of March 16, 1945, to Wise. Roosevelt reaffirmed that he had made clear his support for the Zionist program during the presidential campaign. "That position I have not changed," the president wrote, "and I shall continue to seek to bring about its [the Democratic platform plank on Palestine] earliest realization." [38] Not only did Truman's standing with Zionists sink as a result of his political association with the now somewhat suspect Roosevelt administration, but many Zionists were further disheartened when the president failed to discount the importance of the pledge to the Saudi Arabian monarch. [39]

Although he supported Jewish immigration into Palestine, Truman was hesitant about further antagonizing Arab-American relations by discrediting Roosevelt's letter. [40] Amir Abdullah of Trans-Jordan sent a telegram to the president in which he criticized Truman for sponsoring the immigration of Jews into Palestine. Truman emphasized in his reply to Abdullah that he had not accepted the full Zionist program. By supporting the immigration of 100,000 Jewish refugees, the president wrote, he was in no way prejudicing a decision involving Palestine's future. Nor would the United States favor any change "respecting the basic situation" in Palestine "without full consultation with both Arabs and Jews." [41]

ANGLO-AMERICAN COMMITTEE
ON REFUGEES

Downing Street waited seven weeks before responding on October 19, 1945, to the president's appeal to open Palestine to Jewish refugees. Although the note indicated a willingness to investigate the question of immigration, the British made it clear that for the immediate future the existing regulations would stand. To oppose the Arabs on this issue, the document claimed, would "probably cause serious disturbances throughout the Middle East. . . ." Rather than take any action without further study, the British proposed establishing an Anglo-American inquiry into the problems of Palestine. Jewish immigration into the Holy Land would be one of many issues that the committee would consider. Although skeptical of the delay implicit in accepting the plan, Truman did believe that a commission might find a solution to the refugee problem that would satisfy London. Aware of the importance of acting swiftly in order to salvage Europe's remaining Jews, the president wanted to make sure that the United States did not "become a party to any dilatory tactics." Truman, however, was convinced that the British were interested in finding an equitable solution to the refugee problem, and that they would accept a reasonable proposal by the joint commission.[42]

Attlee and Foreign Secretary Ernest Bevin were clearly stalling for time on the refugee question. One function the inquiry could serve, as far as the British were concerned, would be to postpone for five months the unpleasant decision to deny Jewish displaced persons the right to enter Palestine.[43] While the commission deliberated, the British were spared the stinging criticism that reemerged once the recommended immigration proposals were summarily rejected. Attlee and Bevin were evidently more interested in maintaining Arab friendship than in providing a home for war-ravaged Jews.

Formation of the Anglo-American Committee of Inquiry was publicly announced on November 13, 1945. Presidential optimism was somewhat blunted by the negative Zionist reaction. The American Zionist Emergency Council's co-chairmen, Rabbis Silver and Wise, warned Truman that he had "fallen into a carefully prepared trap" set by Great Britain. Since the president had already stated his policy regarding Jewish immigration, Zionists challenged the usefulness of forming a commission to find a solution to the problem.[44] Silver and Wise predicted that the inquiry would "bring the solution not one step nearer," and would lead to "interminable delays." [45]

Britain and the United States each appointed six members to the committee, which began its work on January 4, 1946.[46] It was not long before commission members who were sympathetic toward Jewish immigration clashed with the State Department representatives assigned to the American delegation. The department, which consistently had been hostile to Jewish claims in the Middle East, found an implacable foe in Bartley Crum, a San Francisco lawyer serving on the committee.[47]

Rumors reached the president in mid-March that Crum was so irritated by State Department advisers that he was prepared to resign. Truman had taken the gamble that the commission could succeed, and he was "very much upset" when he learned of the possible resignation.[48] Because of Crum's support for the Zionist position, his disaffiliation was seen as endangering Jewish acceptance of the committee's recommendations. On March 20, Truman asked David Niles, an administrative assistant to the president, to contact Crum, Niles's personal friend, and urge him to remain a member of the American delegation. Niles informed Crum of the president's concern, and added, "I know you are a good sport and will see it through. . . ."[49] Crum stayed, and the limited legitimacy the inquiry enjoyed among Zionists remained intact. What little enthusiasm the Zionists had for the committee was sure to be diminished even further if the member they most trusted resigned in protest.

Concluding nearly four months of investigation in Europe and the Middle East, the Anglo-American committee signed its report on April 20.[50] All twelve members recommended that Britain "authorize immediately" the admission of 100,-000 Jews into Palestine. The committee asked that "actual immigration be pushed forward as rapidly as conditions will permit." Noting that the war had ended nearly a year before, the commission expressed its concern that most of the Jewish survivors in Europe were still living in wretched conditions on the sites of the former concentration camps. Commenting on the future government of Palestine, the committee was opposed to either a Jewish or an Arab state. It proposed that the British mandate be continued, and that eventually the United Nations should sponsor a trusteeship agreement. Palestine, according to the report, should become "a country in which the legitimate national aspirations of both Jews and Arabs can be reconciled without either side fearing the ascendancy of the other." [51]

By acting on the report, the British had an opportunity to make a significant move toward solving the lamentable refugee problem. Britain's acceptance would also enhance Truman's stature among the Zionists, who had questioned the efficacy of the committee in the first place. The president, pleased that the inquiry had performed its function so well, awaited England's endorsement of the group's work.

A DEFEAT IN CONGRESS

Certainly by the spring of 1946 Truman was eager to receive any encouraging news related to the Palestine matter. British acceptance of the committee's immigration proposal would offset a rout the president suffered the previous December in Congress. A number of United States senators favorable to the Zionist program wanted to put Congress on record in favor of the Zionist goals. Accordingly, a Palestine resolution was introduced by two staunch supporters of the Jewish cause in the Middle East, Senators Robert Wagner and Robert Taft. The resolution called upon the United States government to "use its good offices" in behalf of opening Palestine to "the free entry of Jews" and to assist in establishing "the Jewish national home" there. [52]

Wagner telephoned the White House on October 24, 1945, leaving a message for Truman. The New York Democrat said that unless the president vigorously backed the resolution, Republicans would be able to turn their support for the measure into political capital. [53] Wanting the Anglo-American committee to begin its work with complete freedom of choice, Truman opposed the resolution. Explaining his position at a press conference, the president said that if the "resolution is passed, there isn't any use trying to have a factfinding commission finding facts and making recommendations." [54] A number of senators, including prominent Democrats, continued to press for adoption despite presidential resistance. Writing to Wagner on December 10, Truman stated that "the [Anglo-American] Commission will serve a useful purpose . . . [and] any resolution by the Congress would be more effective after the Commission has made its study." [55] Secretary of State Byrnes contacted congressional leaders and pleaded with them not to tie the hands of the president and the commission by passing the resolution.[56]

Ignoring the appeals, the Senate Foreign Relations Committee approved the resolution by a vote of seventeen to one, and sent it on to full Senate debate. The one dissenting vote was cast by committee chairman Tom Connally, who bitterly commented that Truman had made it clear "to me and the Committee" that it was the wrong time for passage.[57] Four days later, on December 17, the United States Senate voted to endorse the establishment of a Jewish "home" in Palestine. The voice vote consisted of a "crescendo of 'yeas' " followed by "the single, drawled 'no' " of Senator Connally.[58] When the House of Representatives followed the lead of the Senate and adopted the Palestine resolution two days later by a one-sided voice vote, the rebuke of the president was complete.[59] It had long been a Zionist strategy to cultivate congressional sympathy for a Jewish state. The American Zionist Emergency Council from the outset had directed its local affiliates to establish direct contact with their congressmen. The purpose of such contacts, according to a 1943 confidential memorandum from AZEC, was "to produce in this country what already exists in the British House of Commons, a group of national legislators who are familiar with the details of the Palestine situation and can discuss it intelligently." Local AZEC committees were instructed to either send delegations and communications to Washington or set up "small functions" honoring the congressmen when they were in their home districts.[60] The Zionists' tactic to build up support for their program among congressmen had clearly paid off with the passage of the Palestine resolution.

3

British and Arab Resistance

REACTION TO THE REPORT

When the recommendations of the Anglo-American committee were announced, the strongest reaction came from the Arabs. Arguing that an Arab state should rise in Palestine, and that other nations should share the responsibility of providing a home for Jewish refugees, Arab spokesmen unequivocally condemned the committee's suggestions. King ibn-Saud charged the committee with "betrayal," [1] while a Palestinian Arab leader warned the West that if they dared to implement the report, "we will grab at any straw—Russia or anyone who will help us." [2] The Zionists enthusiastically endorsed the proposal for the immigration of 100,000 homeless Jews, but criticized the committee's opposition to a Jewish state.[3] Regardless of this reservation, the Zionist leadership wanted Britain to take the first step in implementation by opening Palestine to the refugees.[4]

For six months the president had maintained that a solution to the problem of Jewish displaced persons could result from the work of the inquiry. Truman endorsed the committee's proposal of Jewish immigration and urged England to allow the refugees to enter with "the greatest dispatch." [5] He would soon discover that his standing among Jews would depend on actual implementation of the committee's immigration recommendation.

Writing to Attlee on May 8, 1946, the president said that the report pointed in the right direction and that he hoped Britain would start lifting the bars to immigration. Attlee replied that delicate negotiations with Egypt were then in progress and that he desired more time before deciding his nation's policy. Having successfully negotiated one treaty, which granted independence to Trans-Jordan, the British had just offered to withdraw all forces from Egypt in exchange for an alliance sanctioning Anglo-Egyptian military arrangements. Egypt eventually rejected the proposal. Although he was not pleased with the additional delay, Truman agreed to wait until May 20.[6]

London's initial reaction to the committee's work discouraged Truman. Before Britain would act on the recommendations, Attlee told the House of Commons, the United States would be asked to share the additional military and financial responsibilities that would be involved. Attlee also said that Britain would not consider allowing large-scale immigration until the illegal Jewish defense units in Palestine were disarmed.[7] Since these combined forces were estimated to be 60,000 strong, and were fiercely independent, there was little hope of disarming them without time-consuming effort.

Any request for American troops was doomed to rejection. In his memoirs, Truman indicates he was under pressure from the Joint Chiefs of Staff not to commit any United States armed forces to Palestine. The use of American troops to enforce the committee's findings, argued the Joint Chiefs, would so embitter the Arabs that Russia might replace the United States and Britain in power and influence throughout the Middle East. Stressing the need to control the area's oil, they concluded that America's vital security interest militated against any action hostile to the Arab world.[8]

On May 27, 1946, one month after the Anglo-American committee finished its work, Attlee called Truman and suggested convening a series of Anglo-American conferences to discuss the report. The prime minister outlined forty-three specific subjects that would be studied. In his response the president said that he would be willing to enter such deliberations, but only after Britain acted to implement the top-priority recommendation involving immigration. Because of the necessity for immediate action, Truman offered Attlee American assistance in transporting the Jewish refugees and housing them in Palestine. Attlee replied that he was not interested in discussing the issue of the 100,000 separately, but instead wished to talk about every aspect of the Palestine problem.[9]

Initial Zionist sympathy with Truman's efforts to get the report implemented rapidly waned as the British stalled. Wise and Silver, in a reply to a State Department request for the American Zionist Emergency Council's comment on the committee report, criticized the delay and called for immediate action to save the surviving remnants of Europe's Jewry. In their letter to Secretary of State James Byrnes, which was also publicly released, the AZEC co-chairmen coolly warned that "further consultations and comments appear meaningless, except to produce delay where immediate action is called for, and to confuse where the issue has long been altogether clear." [10] Disenchantment with the president over the delay, on the part both of Zionists and of a number of outspoken United States senators, presumably played a role in Truman's effort to assign the blame elsewhere. Just two days after the AZEC letter had been made public, the president told a June 6 news conference that Britain, not the United States, was responsible for the seemingly endless postponements.[11]

A week later, Foreign Secretary Bevin publicly stated what had become increasingly apparent for six weeks: Britain had no intention of admitting 100,000 Jews into Palestine, regardless of the committee recommendation. Having invested time and money in cultivating Arab friendship, the British were not about to alienate their strategically important allies. The postwar empire was in enough difficulty without a threatened loss of the Suez Canal and the oil of the Middle East. Bevin said that if Britain allowed Jewish refugees to enter Palestine, "I would have to put another division of British troops in there, and I am not prepared to do it." [12] The Arabs had bluntly insisted that the recommendations of the committee were unacceptable, and would be challenged with their armies if it were necessary.[13] Britain desired to strengthen her alliance with the nations in the Middle East, not oppose them on a battlefield. Frankly annoyed with American policy, Bevin bitterly suggested that the "agitation in the United States, and particularly in New York" for immigration into Palestine "was because they did not want too many of them [Jewish refugees] in New York." The American Zionist Emergency Council's Silver responded by telling a mass protest rally that Bevin was guilty of "anti-Semitic vulgarity reminiscent of the Nazis at their worst." [14]

A NEW ANGLO-AMERICAN STUDY

Discouraged by the ever-increasing gulf that separated England from the Zionists, Truman nevertheless hoped for a solution based upon the committee's recommendations. Accordingly, the president agreed to appoint a cabinet committee that would discuss the Anglo-American committee's findings with a British delegation.[15] Truman's cabinet committee, composed of representatives of the secretaries of state, war, and the treasury, deliberated for two weeks in July with their British counterparts.

By the time the cabinet committee began its work on July 10, 1946, already hostile British-Jewish relations had been further strained. Britain's reluctance to allow immigration was the signal for the illegal Jewish armed forces in Palestine to step up their acts of terrorism against the mandatory power. Britain did not stop at the arrests of persons known to have connections with the illegal elements. On June 29 a drastic retaliation occurred when the British imprisoned the leadership of the Jewish Agency for Palestine, the internationally recognized Zionist organization in Palestine. Attlee attempted to justify this extraordinary action by charging that the Jewish

Agency was secretly conniving with the largest underground
military force in Palestine, the Haganah. Initially formed to
protect Jewish settlements against raids from Arab bands, the
Haganah (the word translates from Hebrew as "defense") had
vigorously opposed terrorism until its membership became
convinced that the British government of Attlee and Bevin
was determined to frustrate the Zionist cause. As far as the
Zionist Emergency Council's leadership was concerned, the
British reaction was "nothing less than an act of war against
the Jewish people." [16]

It was under these strained circumstances that the three-
man American cabinet committee, led by Chairman Henry F.
Grady, met with Great Britain's negotiators. Apparently
Grady was determined that an agreement with the British on
Palestine would be desirable even if it meant large concessions
regarding previous American demands. As late as July 18,
1946, President Truman assured the Jewish Agency that
Grady's committee was "fully advised" of his "feeling of urgency" that Palestine be opened to Jewish refugees.[17] Yet
within a week Grady's group capitulated on this very issue.
The American delegates failed to insist that the immediate immigration of 100,000 Jews into Palestine be made a part of
the arrangement.[18]

Grady and his colleagues returned from their work in London after a security leak enabled the press to publish the committee's recommendations on July 26, 1946. According to the
proposals, Palestine would become a federal state with a central government and separate Jewish and Arab provinces.
Actual power would remain with the central government,
which was to be controlled by Britain. Of more immediate importance, the issue of Jewish immigration into Palestine was
resolved on London's terms. The admission of the 100,000
was made conditional on Arab acceptance of the plan.[19] In effect, Britain would not have to open Palestine to Jews, for the
Arabs would not agree to such a scheme.

As highly as he valued an agreement with the British, the

president could not accept such a blatant capitulation on Jewish immigration. Judge Joseph Hutcheson, chairman of the American delegation of the Anglo-American Committee of Inquiry, bluntly termed the Grady plan a "complete sellout." [20] The advisory staff to Grady's committee was almost unanimously against the manner in which the chairman had handled the immigration question. At least two members of the staff filed strong written protests in opposition to Grady's work.[21] While Arabs opposed the cabinet committee's plan because it sanctioned a Jewish province within Palestine, Zionists were distressed by the elimination of an autonomous Jewish state, as well as by the abandonment of Jewish refugees. The plan was nothing less than a "conscienceless act of treachery," according to Abba Hillel Silver.[22]

Truman was well aware of the political implications were he to endorse Grady's handiwork. Jewish voters might rebel against a president and a political party that could accept such recommendations. Paul Fitzpatrick, chairman of the Democratic State Committee of New York, wired Truman and warned, "If this plan goes into effect it would be useless for the Democrats to nominate a state ticket for the election this fall. I say this without reservation and am certain that my statement can be substantiated." [23] According to a report by *New York Times* writer James Reston, the "political implications of acceptance and rejection were canvassed" by Truman during one cabinet session.[24] Reston also wrote that Truman's political advisers had strongly urged him to oppose Grady's recommendations or force the Democratic party to face severe political consequences.[25] It seems likely that the president's resistance to the cabinet committee's work was in large measure based on the fact that the group so conspicuously failed to provide for Jewish immigration into Palestine. Although Truman did believe that large numbers of Jewish displaced persons should have the right to emigrate to Palestine, it may be presumed that he also acted as he did in order to avoid what he had been informed would be a serious political mistake.

There was never much doubt that the work of the cabinet committee would be found unacceptable and would be rejected. Despite Britain's last-moment threat that refusal to accept the proposals would mean further delay in solving the problems,[26] Truman informed Attlee on August 12, 1946, that the recommendations were not acceptable.[27]

TRUMAN ALIENATES JEWS,
ARABS, AND THE BRITISH

By August 1946, the president's Palestine policy could be considered a complete failure. Secretary of the Navy Forrestal, who had long been concerned that support for refugee immigration into Palestine would damage American interests, wrote that Truman's year-old crusade in favor of large-scale Jewish immigration had alienated many Arabs and caused a drop in American prestige in the Middle East.[28] Ibn-Saud warned Truman that continuation of such a hostile policy could "lead to difficulties and complications the consequences of which only God knows." [29]

Within the Jewish community Truman's reputation had declined precipitously. On August 31, 1945, the president had pledged his support for the immediate immigration of the 100,000; a full year later the doors of Palestine remained locked, and Jewish displaced persons languished in the same camps in which the Nazis had terrorized them. Truman had been warned by the Zionists that Britain sought to postpone a difficult decision, and that by agreeing to the Anglo-American commission the president was legitimizing a protracted stall. The passage of time had proved the Zionist prophecy correct.

Britain also was displeased with Truman's policy. Attlee and Bevin considered their nation's position in the Middle East to be vital to her existence as a world power. Since Arab friendship was understood to be absolutely necessary, Downing Street did not approve of Truman's adamant demands in behalf of Jewish immigration. According to the *New York Times*, Attlee was said to believe that there was a very real possibility that an Arab uprising could result from opening Palestine to Jewish refugees.[30]

In short, the president's policy had managed to alienate Arab, Jew, and Great Britain in varying degrees. As Truman's failure became more apparent, his growing sensitivity on the subject caused moments of anger. James McDonald, one of the Anglo-American committee members, urged the two United States senators from New York (Robert Wagner and James Mead) to join him in calling on the president to protest the cabinet committee findings. McDonald insisted that the proposals agreed to by Grady were a negation of the Anglo-American committee's plan to provide for Jewish immigration to Palestine. During the White House session the president "was so angry with my protests," recounted McDonald, "that he refused to let me read a one-page memorandum of my view." [31] In the fall of 1946 Truman admitted that the problem looked "insoluble." [32] Writing to McDonald, he noted that Palestine provided "a most difficult problem and I have about come to the conclusion that there is no solution, but we will keep trying." Acknowledging his rather obvious display of annoyance during the conference with McDonald and the senators, Truman moved toward more cordial relations by adding, "I hope I wasn't too hard on you." [33]

— 4 —

Truman Sides with the Zionists

ZIONIST EFFORTS
TO WIN PRESIDENTIAL BACKING

In an effort to reverse the tide of increasing tension in the Middle East, Great Britain convened a Palestine conference to attempt to resolve differences between Arab and Jew. The British announced that the conference, which opened in London on September 10, 1946, would have as the basis of discussion the establishment of some type of federated program for Palestine. The *New York Times* reported that even before the initial meeting was held, the Jewish and Arab leadership alike had flatly rejected any federal structure for Palestine. Although Downing Street continued to call for a compromise settlement that would be acceptable to both sides, an overlying pessimism prevailed at the sessions. The Jewish Agency for Palestine, internationally recognized as representing the Palestinian Jews, rejected an invitation to participate formally, and would only consent to private, unofficial negotiations with the British. When the conference did begin, there were no Jewish representatives present.[1] Jewish apprehensions derived from the belief that Attlee and Bevin would never agree to antagonize the Arab world by assenting to any solution acceptable to the Zionists.

Across the Atlantic, Jewish pressure directed at the president reached a fever pitch while the conference went sluggishly about its business. During the fall of 1946, Truman was deluged by "all sorts of pressure . . . to commit American power and forces on behalf of the Jewish aspirations in Palestine." [2] According to James Forrestal, then the secretary of the navy and an outspoken foe of the Zionists, the Jews were "injecting vigorous and active propaganda to force the President's hand with reference to the immediate immigration of Jews into Palestine." [3] Various tactics were adopted in an effort to win Truman's support. Jewish leaders who were able to secure an audience with the president used the opportunity to plead the Zionist case. On several occasions Weizmann was called upon to serve in this capacity. [4] Newspaper advertisements were purchased by Jewish spokesmen in the hope that they would help create a ground swell of public support that would reach the White House. [5] Seemingly endless resolutions, passed by Zionist organizations, called on the president to endorse their program. [6] Mass rallies effectively testified to the enormous public base the Zionists enjoyed. Politicians were advised to take notice when one rally in New York City attracted 150,000 persons. [7] Additional support for the Jewish effort was provided by the many congressmen who continually bombarded Truman with messages urging him to use his presidential power in behalf of some particular part of the Zionist program. [8]

NILES IN THE WHITE HOUSE

Possibly the Zionists' single most important asset in the fall of 1946 was their association with David K. Niles, a member of the president's staff. As an administrative assistant to the president, Niles was able to use his considerable influence within the White House to extend Truman's public support in behalf of the Zionist program. Niles was born into a Jewish family in a Boston slum, and gravitated toward progressive politics in his youth. After he had ably handled administrative posts within the New Deal, Niles was chosen by Roosevelt in 1942 to be one of his administrative assistants. Truman asked

Niles to continue in the same capacity following Roosevelt's death. Niles worked for the new administration as its liaison with the racial and religious minorities, especially with the Jewish community.[9] As the buffer between the president and certain segments of the public, Niles had the task of keeping the latter contented.[10]

Possessing that "passion for anonymity" which President Roosevelt once said all his administrative assistants shared, Niles attempted to avoid public notice or publicity.[11] Not only was he upset when his name appeared in the press, but he also worried that his White House phone might be tapped.[12] During his tenure with the Truman administration, Niles claimed to have little authority. "I am a man of no importance," he once said.[13] On another occasion he was less deprecatory. "I am one of the instruments of the President who has been privileged to give my opinion to the President on Palestine among other things. Decisions are not made by me." [14] Niles was far too modest, for he was indeed influential in helping to mold the president's Palestine policy. Material that arrived at the White House relating to the Palestine issue was sent to Niles for his recommendation or disposition. For example, when Ben H. Freedman cabled the president and asked to speak with him about Palestine, Niles drafted the following reply, although it was sent over the signature of Truman's secretary, Matthew J. Connelly: "The President suggests that you see his Administrative Assistant, . . . Niles, who is familiar with the [subject]. . . ." [15]

What made Niles and his White House connection so valuable to the Zionists was the rapport that existed between leaders of the Jewish movement and the administrative assistant. Niles worked closely with the top echelon of Zionist leadership, the Jewish Agency's Executive. Eliahu Epstein, one member of the Executive, which was the Agency's administrative arm, labeled Niles "our friend" in the White House.[16] Correspondence dealing with Jewish strategy and their battle to win Truman's favor linked Niles with Epstein, Meyer Weisgal, Nahum Goldman, and Stephen Wise, all members of the powerful Executive.[17]

A deliberate effort was made by the Zionist leadership to keep Niles apprised of their every move. Following a private conversation with Lord Inverchapel, the British ambassador to the United States, Goldman wrote a confidential report for distribution to members of the Executive. Goldman also recommended that a copy be sent to Niles for his perusal. Accordingly, Niles was aware that Britain was likely to turn the Palestine problem over to the United Nations at the same time that Zionist leaders learned of the plan.[18] When members of the Executive discovered that Weizmann was threatening to resign from the Jewish Agency over a question of policy, a telegram quickly informed Niles of the organization's internal problem.[19]

Because Niles was cognizant of the exact direction of Zionist policy, and since he was on the president's personal staff, he was in an ideal position to make a direct, sympathetic appeal to Truman on behalf of the Jewish Agency's program. Weizmann later singled Niles out for helping to "bring about a proper understanding of the ideals of our cause in high places in Washington." [20] A striking example of how rapidly the Zionists could influence American policy on Palestine is provided by an incident that occurred in April 1946. Meyer Weisgal, secretary of the Executive, got in touch with Niles and noted that Judge Joseph Hutcheson was maintaining a friendly attitude toward the Jews in his role as chairman of the Anglo-American Committee of Inquiry that was to recommend policies for Palestine. However, added Weisgal, it was essential that "the boss in Washington [Truman] should cable him, encouraging him in his stand and expressing confidence in his efforts to bring about a quick solution of the whole problem." Within a few days Niles drafted such a telegram and then recommended to Truman that he send the message to Hutcheson. Two days later the president assented to the advice of his aide, and the dispatch was transmitted to Hutcheson.[21]

Niles was also able to influence the direction of Zionist policy because of his close ties with the Jewish leadership. When a confidential State Department memorandum informed him that certain Jews were attempting to block a proposed American loan to Britain, Niles helped to quell these activities by securing statements from Zionist leaders in favor of the loan. According to Francis Russell, representing the department's Office of Public Information, the State Department learned that several major American Zionist groups were considering an effort to defeat or at least delay the British loan. Russell told Niles that the department had learned that the "basic strategy" of the groups, which were said to include AZEC, would be "to use their opposition to the loan to get concessions from the British with respect to Palestine. . . ." [22] When the administration needed to obtain statements by prominent Zionists in order to forestall the threatened campaign against the loan, Niles promised to line up the appropriate endorsements. [23] Among those who responded to Niles's request for support was Rabbi Stephen Wise, one of the most respected Zionist leaders. [24]

A memorandum Niles wrote for the president on May 27, 1946, provides an excellent example of his advocacy of a pro-Zionist policy and his ability to use his position to insure that the Zionist cause received a sympathetic hearing by the chief executive. Niles advised Truman not to be deterred from supporting Jewish claims for fear of losing the friendship of the king of Saudi Arabia. "You know that President Roosevelt said to some of us privately he could do anything that needed to be done with Ibn Saud with a few million dollars." Niles also recommended that in determining Palestine policy, Truman should not be concerned with threats that the Arabs would violently oppose Zionists aims in the Middle East. "The danger of unifying the Moslem world can be discounted because a good part of the Moslem world follows Gandhi and his philosophy of non-resistance." An American delegate on the Anglo-American committee, Frank Buxton, was reported by Niles to have "told me . . . that he had talked privately with many Arab Chiefs who said that outside of a few minor incidents there really would be very little opposition." The conclusion of Niles's memorandum was an appeal for the immediate immigration into Palestine of 100,000 Jews. These refugees "would be of great assistance to us in the area as the Jews of Palestine were during the second World War, which is generally admitted by everybody who is familiar with the situation." America and the other allied forces "got no help from the Arabs at all but considerable help from the Jews in Palestine." [25]

For one who so ardently argued the Zionist cause at the highest level of government, the accolades Niles received were well deserved. Moshe Sharett, while serving as the Israeli foreign minister, reflected on the "inestimable assistance" and "far-reaching effectiveness" of Niles's White House labors.[26] Opponents of the establishment of a Jewish state were far from enthusiastic, but they were conscious of Niles's significance. Forrestal noted that the State Department was "seriously embarrassed and handicapped by the activities of Niles at the White House in going directly to the President on matters involving Palestine." [27]

TRUMAN'S COMMITMENT OF 1946

With the November 1946 election not far off, nervous warnings were heard within the Democratic party that there would be trouble unless the president effected a political rapprochement with the disenchanted Jewish community. Truman, as well as his political advisers, grew increasingly sensitive toward this potentially explosive issue and they tended to insulate themselves from the diverse pressures in the American Jewish community.[28] Brooklyn Representative Emanuel Celler, a Jewish leader, attempted to arrange a session between New York State's congressional delegation and the president in

order to impress upon Truman the extent of pro-Zionist sentiment in the state. Celler telephoned the White House several
times, but Truman flatly refused to meet with the group. For a
while Niles avoided a direct confrontation with Celler over
the issue by engaging in a policy of evasion and not informing
the congressman of Truman's adamant refusal to be brought
under additional pressure.[29] The angered Celler wrote Truman
that he was "rather startled" by the rebuff. The president's actions, he stated, "certainly will give political ammunition to
the upstate Republicans who wanted to attend and you remem-
ber that New York faces a very crucial election." Celler added
that he felt "it is bad politics for the President not to meet
with them—even if it is on the Palestine question." [30]

Truman did eventually agree to the session, but throughout
it he was inattentive. At one point he expressed his annoyance
with what he suggested was the political reason for the visit.
He continually shuffled the papers in front of him, and even
interrupted Celler's comments and said that he did not have
time to listen. Although he realized that the congressmen were
up for reelection, the president said, he wished that people
would come to see him about the country's problems, not
their own. Before the delegation was ready to leave, Truman
abruptly terminated the meeting.[31]

At the same time that Truman received the New York delegation, Great Britain was preparing to convene the London
conference. Shortly after the conference began on September
10, 1946, Eliahu Epstein renewed his conversations with
Niles. Epstein, a member of the Jewish Agency Executive and
the Agency's Washington representative, informed Niles that a
deadlock had been reached in the agency's unofficial discussions with the British. No longer could the president's actions
fairly be interpreted as damaging chances for a London settlement. On approximately the same date, Stephen Wise conferred
with the president and "stimulated [Truman] to a renewed attempt on the Palestine problems of which he was ready to

wash his hands after the crisis resulting from the failure of the Grady mission." [32]

It soon became clear that what the Zionists sought was an unequivocal statement by the president supporting the establishment of a Jewish state in Palestine. While Wise was sparking Truman's interest in taking a positive stand, Bartley Crum attempted to persuade the chairman of the Democratic National Committee of the need for a pro-Zionist declaration. Crum "worked hard on [Robert E.] Hannegan [the chairman] and finally obtained his support in the matter." What swayed Hannegan was a letter from Crum, apparently emphasizing the positive political implications of a presidential statement favorable to the Jews. Epstein, who consulted frequently with Niles "during the critical days preceding the statement," applauded the administrative assistant for his unwavering cooperation and noted that the letter from Crum that finally convinced Hannegan "was inspired by our friend [Niles] and even written in his office." Niles was thus able to convince Truman that the Republican candidates, particularly in New York, in the upcoming election "overtly showed their determination to make the Palestine issue one of the focal points of attack on Truman and the Democratic Administration." [33] Niles warned that unless the president countered an expected pro-Zionist statement by Governor Thomas Dewey, and spoke out himself, New York State would surely be lost to the Democrats. [34]

Opposition to Niles came from the State Department. On September 12, 1946, William Clayton, the acting secretary of state, wrote Truman and warned that Wise and others would attempt to secure a statement favoring a Jewish state. Within the department, Clayton emphasized, "we do not feel that it would be advisable for you to issue such a statement at this time." Clayton added that a concession on this point would "merely be encouraging them [presumably the Zionist leadership] to make fresh demands and to apply pressures in the fu-

ture." Truman was also reminded that the Joint Chiefs of
Staff "have urged that we take no action with regard to Palestine which might orient the peoples of the entire area away
from the Western Powers. . . ." [35] In reply the president confided that he had "been very hesitant about saying anything on
the subject. I hope it will not be necessary for me to have anything to say." [36]

Clayton's appeal was to no avail, for by early October Niles
had, at the very least, convinced Truman of the political necessity for an immediate commitment to the Jewish community. The president finally issued his statement on the most
sacred day in the Hebrew religious calendar, Yom Kippur.
Truman not only reiterated his call for "substantial immigration into Palestine . . . at once," but of far greater significance, he endorsed the establishment of "a viable Jewish
state" in Palestine. [37] For the first time since he assumed office,
the president was on record as supporting the basic Zionist
goal.

Truman had momentarily stolen the initiative from Dewey,
who was already scheduled to speak on Palestine two days
later. Since the Republican leader had long been in favor of a
Jewish state, his appeal to the electorate consisted of challenging Truman's support for the immigration of 100,000 refugees. Dewey demanded that "it must be an immigration not of
100,000, but of several hundreds of thousands." [38] The Zionists watched with satisfaction as the two party leaders tried to
outbid each other in an attempt to win favor among Jewish
voters.

Democrats, especially in New York, were jubilant over the
timing of the president's declaration, coming as it did just a
month before the election. Celler complimented Truman on
his stand, and noted that it was also likely to have a "very desirable political effect upon our chances in New York." [39]
Hannegan happily discovered that Truman's stature among
Jews was visibly improved as a result of the statement. [40]

Downing Street was less than enthusiastic over the course

of events. One government spokesman charged that Truman's actions "may well jeopardize" the effort taking place in London to find a compromise settlement between Arab and Jew.[41] According to Eliahu Epstein, the British used Truman's declaration to excuse their own inability to find a solution. Prior to the presidential statement the unofficial British-Jewish negotiations going on in London had reached a dead end.[42]

Although the Zionist leaders publicly applauded Truman's stand, a surprisingly large number of them expressed concern over some of the president's wording. These fears proved groundless, but they exposed a rift between the Zionists who staunchly defended Truman and those who had reservations about him.[43] Stephen Wise, a Truman supporter, was so irritated by what he felt was a lack of appreciation on the part of his colleagues that he decided to withdraw as co-chairman of the American Zionist Emergency Council.[44] Having toiled long and hard for this commitment, the Zionists were determined to keep Truman loyal to their cause. Epstein pointedly remarked that those "behind the struggle for a Jewish Palestine . . . will not let President Truman make of it [his Yom Kippur statement] a mere pre-election statement even if he would like to do so." [45]

An expected indignant response toward Truman's action came from the Arab leadership. The Arab Higher Committee insisted that Truman's action "clearly reveals that American policy is directed against the Arab people of Palestine and thereby against all Arabs who support their brethren here." [46] King ibn-Saud charged Truman with "contradicting his previous promises" by not consulting with all the parties involved before calling for an alteration of the basic situation in Palestine.[47] Any Zionist doubts that Truman was hedging on his support for a Jewish state in his October 4 statement were dispelled by the president's firm reply to the Saudi Arabian monarch. In a letter that was released to the press, Truman outlined his Palestine policy, which included large-scale immigration and the establishment of a Jewish national home.[48] As far as the Jewish Agency was concerned, Truman's blunt message to the Arab king was a "source of deep comfort." [49]

Yet from the point of view of domestic politics, the Democratic strategy of appealing to Jewish voters never had a chance to work in 1946. A decisive Republican triumph was in the making and not even in New York State did the Democrats survive the political landslide by clinging to their president's last-moment effort to please the Jews. Effectively charging the incumbent Democrats with responsibility for the nation's soaring rate of inflation, the Republican party won solid control of both the House of Representatives and the Senate for the first time since 1928. Republicans also captured the governorships in twenty-five of the thirty-two non-Southern states. Aside from the crucial inflation issue, Democrats were placed on the defensive by positions taken by the Truman administration. The president lost a significant amount of organized labor support through his unfriendly treatment of John L. Lewis and his breaking of the 1946 railroad strike. Many of Roosevelt's followers reacted negatively to the abrupt departure from Truman's cabinet of two staunch New Dealers, Henry A. Wallace and Harold L. Ickes. What is more, Democrats could not counter losses among New Dealers and organized labor, by courting more conservative voters, since the president's civil rights and welfare programs had already firmly alienated this latter group.

A week after the election, Forrestal visited Truman and recommended that from then on Palestine be handled in a nonpartisan manner. Forrestal was discouraged by how difficult the prospects appeared to be for taking Palestine "out of politics." According to Forrestal, Truman "seems to feel that not much will come of such an attempt, that political maneuvering is inevitable, politics and our government being what they are." [50] Future events would confirm the president's judgment.

5

Britain Goes to the United Nations

FAILURE TO BREAK
THE IMPASSE IN LONDON

During the winter of 1946–47, Attlee and Bevin found themselves in an awkward position. The two British leaders were responsible for a policy that denied to the survivors of the most victimized people of World War II an opportunity to begin a new life. Yet the decisions leading to this result were made with full awareness, for it was believed that any other course of action would endanger Great Britain's national security. British policy aimed at uniting the Arab nations in an alliance that would help preserve London's interests. Continued access to Arab oil, a secure route to the East, and an unyielding opposition to Soviet penetration of the Middle East were of particular importance to Attlee and Bevin.[1]

Great Britain was not about to become a partner to any imposed settlement hostile to the Arabs. Instead, the government held a slender hope that the London conference would somehow arrive at a compromise palatable to both protagonists in the hitherto insoluble Palestine deadlock. However, the irreducible minimums that the parties would tolerate were far apart. Arab spokesmen refused to sanction substantial immigration of refugees, much less assent to any Jewish autonomy in Palestine. According to Charles E. Egan, the *New York Times* reporter covering the London conference, the "unexpectedly violent reaction of Arabs against any suggestions of partition in Palestine have stunned Bevin and other top offi-

cials in the Foreign and Colonial Offices." The head of the
Palestinian Arab delegation, Jamal el Husseini, informed
Egan that "war was certain to break out if Britain tried to impose a partition plan." [2] For its part the Jewish Agency made
it clear that the only basis on which it would negotiate in London would be a plan which would establish some sort of Jewish state in Palestine. Moshe Shertok, a spokesman for the
Jewish Agency for Palestine, announced that the agency had
notified Bevin even before the meetings began that the "only
basis on which it would confer was the re-establishment of the
'Jewish national home' in Palestine, which meant the creation
of an independent Zionist state through partition." [3] On February 9, 1947, the conference collapsed when it became obvious that Britain could not find an acceptable basis for discussion. According to Egan's dispatches, the British offered
their final compromise plan for discussion on February 7. The
plan was reported to have proposed the establishment of
semi-autonomous Jewish and Arab states. These semi-autonomous states were to be reviewed after five years, with no guarantee that permanent partition would be the next step. On
February 8 both the Arabs and the Jews expressed their complete disapproval of the compromise plan. The conference
reached its end on February 9, when, according to Egan,
"both Zionists and Arabs hardened their opposition to the
new British proposal." [4]

One Western observer sees Arab hostility toward massive
Jewish immigration as based on a fear that additional Jews
would displace the indigenous population. According to the
Palestinian Arabs, the Zionists intended eventually to remove
the Arabs from the Holy Land. The Arabs believed that following the Nazi terror in Europe, shamed gentiles wished to
make amends for centuries of Jewish mistreatment in the West.
By sanctioning Zionist designs in Palestine, the Western powers
were viewed by Arabs as ordering the natives to accede to
physical eviction to pay for crimes of which they were inno-
cent.[5]

Ernest Bevin, the foreign secretary who directed Britain's

role at the conference, spoke bitterly of the "unreason-
ableness" of both Arab and Jew.[6] On February 14, 1947, he
formally announced that his government had failed to come
up with a solution, and that Great Britain would refer the
whole Palestine problem to the United Nations.[7] In a callous
reference to the Jewish refugees who now faced additional
delay before their future would be determined, Bevin remarked that "after two thousand years of conflict, another
twelve months will not be considered a long delay." [8]

During a heated debate in the House of Commons on February 25, 1947, Bevin elaborated on the reasons why the conference had failed. Although a few days earlier he had stressed
the near impossibility of bringing the Jews and Arabs together, Bevin now spoke of the conference in far different
terms. According to the foreign secretary, the London sessions
were on the verge of a settlement when they were undercut by
the president of the United States. "I had the right approach
at last," Bevin argued, when a telephone call from Attlee informed him of the statement that Truman was going to issue
the next day, October 4, 1946. Bevin talked with Secretary of
State Byrnes and appealed to him to stop the declaration from
being announced. "I believed we were on the road if only they
would leave us alone. I begged that the statement should not
be issued but I was told that if it was not issued by Mr. Truman, a competitive statement would be issued by Mr.
Dewey." In his capacity as foreign secretary, Bevin continued,
he was seriously handicapped in handling international affairs
"if my problem is made the subject of local elections." Although a Palestine solution had seemed possible, Truman's
"statement was issued . . . and the whole thing was spoiled."
According to Bevin, Truman was also to blame for the minimal number of Jewish refugees that Britain had allowed to
enter Palestine. A larger number of displaced persons could
have been accommodated "if the bitterness of feeling had not
been increased by American pressure for the immediate decision on 100,000." [9]

Bevin's angry observations were aimed at quieting the

swelling criticism in Britain that had emerged over his handling of the Palestine issue. Correspondent Egan wrote that he
had learned that Bevin's strong language had received Attlee's
prior approval: "It was authoritatively disclosed that Bevin's
speech had Prime Minister Attlee's full backing. It is emphasized the remarks were far from being extemporaneous
charges uttered in the heat of debate but had been checked
with Mr. Attlee in advance." [10] It was unfair to blame the col-
lapse of negotiations on Truman, however, for the London
conference was never even remotely on the verge of a solution. Nahum Goldman, one of the Jewish Agency's key negotiators during the unofficial discussions in London, bluntly
commented, "There was never a moment in all our conversations in which there was the possibility of agreement." Another representative of the agency, Moshe Sharett, agreed that
there was absolutely no basis for discussion and no possible
prospect of solution.[11] By the time Truman made his Yom
Kippur statement on October 4, 1946, it was clear that the
London conference was going nowhere.[12]

Truman was "outraged" when he learned of Bevin's personal assault.[13] He did, however, reject Byrnes's proposal for
a statement criticizing the foreign secretary by name.[14] The
president instead issued a more impersonal note, without mention of Bevin, saying that he wished to correct the "most unfortunate and misleading" remarks that had been expressed.
Truman denied any responsibility for the failure of the conference, and he also claimed that local politics had not influ-
enced his decision to issue the statement of October 4.[15]

As a result of Bevin's intemperate attack, Truman found
himself being staunchly defended within the Jewish community. To be orally assailed by the foreign secretary, a man the
Zionists hated, inadvertently made a sympathetic figure of the
president in Jewish eyes.[16] White House public opinion mail
overwhelmingly defended Truman, and congressional response to the incident also favored the chief executive. Senators Homer E. Capehart, Robert A. Taft, Alben W. Barkley,

and Herbert H. Lehman strongly criticized Bevin's remarks. Lehman said: "The words spoken by Mr. Bevin are not those of a statesman. They are petulant, uninformed, and disingenuous." Representative Sol Bloom, former chairman of the House Foreign Affairs Committee, said Bevin was "stupid, stupid, stupid. He just doesn't know what he's talking about. Everything he said is just not true." Representative Emanuel Celler insisted that the foreign secretary's statement was "a damnable lie." [17]

FORMATION OF A UNITED NATIONS STUDY COMMISSION

On April 2, 1947, Great Britain formally asked the United Nations to summon a special session of the General Assembly. Secretary-General Trygve Lie arranged for the full membership of the General Assembly to meet at Lake Success, New York, in late April for an extraordinary session to consider the Palestine problem. Britain recommended that the session limit itself to appointing a fact-finding commission that would investigate the problem, and then present a report at the regular meeting in September. Since the United Nations honored the League of Nations mandates, Great Britain's position in Palestine was still authorized. According to the United Nations Charter, the mandate would remain in force until Britain decided to relinquish the territory to the United Nations trusteeship system. The General Assembly could only recommend a solution, and the final determination on Palestine's future would have to be made by Downing Street.[18] While the United Nations deliberated, Britain would continue to retain the mandate for Palestine.

When the special session opened on April 23, 1947, the American delegation backed Britain's proposal to establish a study commission and then adjourn.[19] A difficulty in executing this plan arose when the Zionists lobbied for an opportunity to present their case at the extraordinary session.[20] A compromise arrangement, supported by both the United States and Great Britain, instructed the General Assembly's Political and Security Committee to give both the Jewish Agency and the official spokesmen for the Palestinian Arabs, the Arab Higher Committee, a hearing.[21] After formally establishing an eleven-nation commission of inquiry to study the Palestine problem and submit proposals for its solution, the United Nations session adjourned on May 15, 1947.[22]

Truman did not want the United States to influence the commission's work. The president believed that if the inquiry was given a free hand, it would stand a better chance of finding a solution. Secretary of State George Marshall was quoted by the *New York Times* as saying that it would be "premature" for the United States to work in behalf of the adoption of one plan or another. During a cabinet meeting on August 8, 1947, Truman announced that he wanted to wait until the United Nations had finished its investigation before he would make a commitment. According to Forrestal's diary, "The President interjected at this time that he proposed to make no announcements or statements upon the Palestine situation until after the United Nations had made its findings. He said he had stuck his neck out on this delicate question once, and he did not propose to do it again." [23] When Senator Robert Wagner questioned what appeared to be the American policy of neutrality, the State Department replied: "It would be premature for the Government to develop its policy with regard to the substance of [the Palestine] question in such a way as to limit the full utilization of [the] Commission's recommendations and its report." [24]

Irked and discouraged by the government's position, the Zionists argued that Truman had unalterably committed himself to the Jewish Agency's program in his Yom Kippur statement. The Zionists expected that the president would vigorously lead the campaign in the United Nations for large-scale immigration and establishment of a Jewish state in Palestine, rather than stand back and wait for the commission report. Dr. Emanuel Neumann, president of the Zionist Organization of America, said that the United States government's silence was "in effect throwing the game to the adversaries." The chairman of the American Zionist Emergency Council, Rabbi Silver, called on Truman to take the lead in bringing about a solution to the Palestine issue that would give justice to the Jews.[25]

While the United Nations' special committee grappled with the Palestine problem during the summer of 1947, a dangerous escalation of bellicosity shook the Middle East. It was late in 1945 when the final immigration certificates issued by Britain were spent, and at that point all legal Jewish immigration into Palestine ceased.[26] During early 1946 the British relented; a new policy stipulated that 1,500 refugees a month could enter.[27] The Jewish Agency considered this figure to be grossly inadequate since approximately one million Jewish displaced persons were still in Europe.[28] With all legal routes closed, a series of antiquated ships loaded with human contraband moved toward the Palestine coast under the protection of night.

Sometimes the ships delivered their live cargo safely to the forbidden shore, but often ugly scenes occurred when the vessels were ensnared by the "Bevin Blockade." More than one refugee, during his fanatical attempt to close the few yards that separated him from the promised land, had been felled by bullets from a British soldier's rifle. The Jews aboard ships that were captured were taken by the British to Cyprus, where they were held in detention camps. There, double rows of high barbed-wire fences, plus the constant watch of two battalions of British troops, kept the refugees in check. German prisoners of war were tactlessly used on Cyprus to build the camps. Jewish refugees on the island were sickened by the fact that the Germans, who were clearly given more personal freedom than the internees, could be viewed circulating outside the camps without guard. By March 1947, it was reported, about 10,500 Jews were in the Cyprus camps amid the familiar terrors of omnipresent guard towers and blinding floodlights.[29]

Bitterness over the detention camps intensified, and eventually provided the Jews in Palestine with the impetus to retaliate. In July 1947 an emotional issue developed that caused the Jewish community to become even more angry with the British. *Exodus, 1947,* a refugee ship with 4,550 persons aboard, came under fire from British destroyers while attempting to land in violation of the law, and after three hours of bloody and vicious conflict was rendered inoperable. Leaving three Jews dead and scores injured, the British immediately transported the others on board to Cyprus. The *Exodus* had been carrying the largest illegal contingent ever to reach Palestine. Now, her sides caved in to reveal a pathetic scene of tiers of bunks and a few scattered belongings,[30] the battered vessel became the very symbol of British treachery to the Jews.

Further exacerbating the Palestine situation were the two major Jewish terrorist groups in Palestine, the Irgun and the Stern group, which were increasingly active against the British and Arabs. In specific retaliation for the hanging of three of their members, the Irgun garroted and then hanged two British army sergeants. Incensed by this incident, a few members of the British military and police streamed through the streets of Tel Aviv with their guns blazing. Before it was over they had indiscriminately killed five Jews and wounded fifteen others.[31] These events during the summer of 1947 put added pressure on the United Nations commission to find a political solution or prepare to watch Palestine explode in continued violence.

TRUMAN UNDER PRESSURE

Truman, fearing that the spiraling cycle of violence in Palestine would make the commission's work more difficult, agreed, on June 5, 1947, to make a statement that was drafted and staunchly endorsed by Secretary of State Marshall. Truman urged "every American citizen . . . to refrain . . . from engaging in, or facilitating, any activities which tend further to inflame the passions of the inhabitants of Palestine, to undermine law and order in Palestine, or to promote violence. . . ." [32] Truman's statement was aimed at those who were publicly raising money in the United States to support the terrorist organizations in Palestine. Great Britain had protested to Washington about the bold newspaper advertisements that sought money to support these groups. [33]

A growing disenchantment with Truman could be detected among Zionist leaders. Responding to the president's criticism of Jewish terrorist activities, the American Zionist Emergency Council coolly noted that "it would be most helpful if the President were also to call upon the Mandatory Government [Britain] to cease those illegal acts which are the very root of the disturbances in Palestine." [34] Eliahu Epstein, the Jewish Agency's Washington representative, had remarked in the wake of Truman's Yom Kippur statement in October 1946 that enough people "will not let President Truman make of it a mere pre-election statement even if he would like to do so." [35] It was clear that the Jewish community was determined not to let the president walk away from his pledge. An intensified mail campaign suggested that Truman direct his attack at Great Britain, not the Jews. [36] He was warned of the dire political consequences he would encounter unless he stood by his promised support. For example, one Zionist group informed the president: "Your policy on Palestine of talking but not acting has cost you our support in 1948." [37]

Truman reacted negatively to the Jewish insistence that he was in debt to them because of a prior commitment. He did not wish to believe that as a result of the Yom Kippur statement he had lost all flexibility on the issue and become locked into an acceptance of the Jewish Agency's proposed program for Palestine. Zionist leaders for their part insisted that when Truman had endorsed the establishment of a "viable Jewish state" in Palestine, he had made a commitment to assist in making the Jewish state a reality. As the Zionists intensified their efforts to remind him of his pledge, the president's anger began to flare. When Truman read one critical letter that accused him of "preferring fascist and Arab elements to the democracy-loving Jewish people of Palestine," he reacted hotly. Requesting that Niles write the response, Truman told his administrative assistant: "It is such drivels [sic] as this that makes Anti-Semites. I thought maybe you had best answer it because I might tell him what's good for him." [38] Zionist leader Stephen Wise, a loyal supporter of the president, appealed to Truman on August 1, 1947, to use his influence to halt the assault on Jews by the British military and police. In a curt, unsympathetic reply, the president pointed out that there seemed to be "two sides to this question. I am finding it rather difficult to decide which one is right and a great many other people in the country are beginning to feel just as I do." [39]

Working from his position on the White House staff, David Niles continued to be a valuable ally of the Zionists. On July 29, 1947, he wrote a memorandum which suggested a course of action for Truman to follow in regard to the United Nations session that was scheduled to open in September. Niles proposed that the American delegation to the session include personnel who would work to implement the president's publicly stated Palestine policy of large-scale immigration and creation of a Jewish state. There can be little doubt that the administrative assistant was referring to Truman's Yom Kippur statement of October 1946. The United States delegation at the special United Nations meeting that previous spring, Niles noted, had failed to support the president's Palestine policy. According to Niles, the trouble did not lie with the regular membership of that group. Niles wrote in a memorandum:

It lies, I think, with the advisers to the delegation. [Niles had been led to understand that the] key advisers on Palestine to the United States Delegation at the Fall Session will be Loy Henderson and George Wadsworth [two veteran State Department diplomats]. Because both are widely regarded as unsympathetic to the Jewish viewpoint, much resentment will be engendered when their appointment is announced and later. Moreover, on the basis of their past behavior and attitudes, I frankly doubt that they will vigorously carry out your policy [of immigration into Palestine and the establishment of a Jewish state there]. But your administration, not they, will be held responsible.

It may not be feasible to oppose Henderson and Wadsworth as advisers to the Delegation. In any event, I believe it is most important that at least one of the advisers be a vigorous and well-informed individual in whom you, the members of the United States Delegation, and American Jewry have complete confidence. There is only one person I know who could fill the bill completely— [former] General [John H.] Hilldring. As you know, he is scheduled to leave his position as Assistant Secretary of State on the first of September. I respectfully recommend that you ask him as a matter of urgency to serve as an adviser to the United States Delegation to insure that your viewpoint is effectively expressed.[40]

In this same memorandum, Niles commented on the widespread criticism among the Zionists that had been aimed at Loy Henderson. Henderson, director of the State Department's Office of Near Eastern and African Affairs, was a strong foe of any official United States support for Zionism. Bartley Crum, a member of the Anglo-American Committee of Inquiry and close to the Zionist leadership, had charged Henderson with frustrating the president's Palestine policy. Concerning Henderson, Niles's memorandum read:

. . . as you so well know, our temperamental friends, headed up by such people as Bart Crum and [AZEC's Rabbi Abba Hillel] Silver continue to spread the stories that Loy Henderson . . . continues to misinterpret your policy. Henderson has not yet, in my judgement, satisfactorily answered the charges made against him by Bart Crum. I think that

Bart Crum was wrong in making these charges, but I do not think the State Department handled any reply in a way that has removed suspicion from Henderson himself.[41]

On September 19, 1947, Hilldring, a former military officer who had been a consistent proponent of the Zionist program for many years, was formally appointed by Truman to the United States delegation as a special adviser on the Palestine issue.[42]

UNSCOP AND THE PROPOSED PARTITION OF PALESTINE

While the American delegation for the regular September session was being selected, the United Nations Special Committee on Palestine was preparing the report which had been authorized by the General Assembly. Representatives from the eleven member-nations deliberated from May 26 until August 31, 1947.[43] Chances for a settlement suffered a setback when the Arab Higher Committee, representing the Palestinian Arabs, refused to offer any cooperation and boycotted UNSCOP's meetings.[44] Spokesmen for the Arab states ominously told the inquiry that an attempt to set up a Jewish state would mean war in the Middle East. In a terse joint declaration, six of the seven Arab League nations made it clear that their governments would resist with whatever violence would be necessary the establishment of such a state.[45] Rather than give up an opportunity to help mold UNSCOP's decision, the Jewish Agency for Palestine attempted to influence the committee's recommendations. Official witnesses formally asked for a Jewish state in all of Palestine, but the Zionists also let it be known that they would accept an offer of less territory as part of a compromise.[46]

On August 31, 1947, UNSCOP issued a report for the consideration of the General Assembly. The committee unanimously agreed that the British mandate in Palestine should be terminated and that some form of independence should be worked out. There was unanimity only on this one point, however. Seven of the eleven members joined in a recommendation that Palestine be partitioned into two independent states, one Jewish and the other Arab. The partition plan contemplated large-scale Jewish immigration and the establishment of a Jewish-Arab economic union.[47] A minority report was written by the representatives of three nations who opposed the partition scheme. The minority plan recommended a federal structure with the Jews and Arabs each retaining control over local affairs in their sector. A bicameral federal legislature was designed to handle national affairs. One house would give equal representation to Jews and Arabs, while the other would be based on population. UNSCOP's report was forwarded to the General Assembly for consideration at its fall, 1947, session.[48]

6

The United Nations Approves Partition

UNITED NATIONS ENDORSEMENT OF PARTITION IN COMMITTEE

On September 23, 1947, the United Nations General Assembly convened at Lake Success, New York, to receive UNSCOP's report. The Ad Hoc Committee on the Palestine Question, consisting of a representative from each United Nations member-state, was set up by the assembly to study UNSCOP's work. Arthur Creech Jones, Britain's colonial secretary, informed the Ad Hoc Committee that his nation was voluntarily laying down its mandate over Palestine. London would accept the United Nations decision concerning the future of the troubled Holy Land. Even if the world organization should fail to reach a settlement, the colonial secretary warned, Britain would still make an early withdrawal of her 100,000 troops. Unless the United Nations ruling on Palestine was acceptable to Jews and Arabs, notice was given that London would not undertake to implement the settlement.[1]

Before the United States would formally commit herself on UNSCOP's partition proposal, Secretary of State Marshall sponsored a final effort to find a compromise solution satisfactory to both Arab and Jew.[2] Any hope for such a settlement, however, vanished in early October 1947, when the Arab League instructed its member states to move troops to the Palestine border for use if Britain should immediately withdraw her forces.[3] This belligerent act convinced Truman that any attempt at that time to obtain a Jewish-Arab rapprochement was doomed. As a result of a direct order from the White House, an endorsement of UNSCOP's partition plan was announced by American delegate Herschel Johnson on October 11, 1947. In a unanimous decision, the governing council of the Arab League recommended that the League's seven member-states send military forces to the Palestine border. According to Clifton Daniel of the *New York Times,* the object was to occupy Palestine should Britain suddenly withdraw, and to resist any Jewish efforts to establish a state. Troop movements were first reported on October 10, and Arab soldiers were sighted at the frontier of Palestine on October 12.[4]

It seems likely that Truman decided to back the partition plan because he viewed it as the only available solution worthy of support in the fall of 1947. Britain had announced her intended withdrawal, and it appeared that a fight between Arabs and Jews could be prevented only by an arrangement imposed by the United Nations. Since the Arabs were adamantly opposed to both the majority plan and the minority plan of UNSCOP, it appeared that American support for the minority, or federal, scheme would have involved approximately the same risks for American interests in the Middle East. The federal proposal, however, did not satisfy the Jews, whereas the majority scheme did command their support.[5] Unnamed American officials at Lake Success were reported by the *New York Times* to have said that one of the primary reasons for Truman's decision was the government's policy of accepting the majority recommendations of United Nations agencies whenever possible.[6] Although probably not the major determinant, the opportunity to endorse a United Nations agency solution, and thereby demonstrate United States support for the world organization, made the president's choice a more acceptable one.

Although the Soviet Union joined the United States in support of partition, this unusual spectacle of cooperation did not alone insure passage in the General Assembly.[7] The Jewish Agency for Palestine was aware that it would be difficult to secure the two-thirds vote necessary to pass the majority plan. Thomas J. Hamilton, the *New York Times* United Nations correspondent, wrote: "It is believed that if the Palestine issue is brought before the General Assembly the combined connections of the Arab bloc would make a decision in favor of the Arabs extremely likely." At an earlier General Assembly session the Arab bloc had combined with the Latin American bloc to guarantee the election of all their candidates to the Economic and Social Council. A coalition of Arab and Latin American states on Palestine would insure the defeat of partition.[8]

Zionists were organized on a global scale by the time the session opened. David Horowitz, an official of the Jewish Agency, characterized the role of the agency's United Nations delegation as "a nerve-center of Zionist diplomacy, its tentacles reaching to all parts of the world." [9] Zionist diplomatic effectiveness was demonstrated during the struggle over the fate of the Negev, a desert area in southern Palestine. America's United Nations delegation argued that the southern part of the Negev should be assigned to the Arab state that was contemplated in the partition proposal. It was the United States position that allotting a section of the Negev to the Arab state would make the partition plan fairer and would thereby make chances for passage more likely. John Hilldring explained that the American delegates believed there should be fewer Arabs assigned to live in the Jewish area and that the two states should be roughly equal in size, not the 60–40 division called for in UNSCOP's majority report. Removing part of the Negev from the Jewish state would remedy both these problems, said Hilldring.[10]

Since the Jews attached great value to ownership of the Negev, Chaim Weizmann was dispatched to Washington to present the Zionist case to Truman. On November 19, 1947, Weizmann visited the president and stressed the opinion of Jewish officials in Palestine that the Negev was destined to become an integral part of their new state once water could be brought to it. Excision of the southern section of the Negev would remove the port at Aqaba from Jewish control. "But for us it was imperative," Weizmann later wrote, that Aqaba be included in the Jewish state. Weizmann told Truman that Aqaba and the surrounding region would perhaps always remain a desert under Arab rule. Should the Jews acquire Aqaba, however, "it will open up a new route for trade and commerce." Since the Egyptians would soon regulate the Suez Canal, an unfriendly Egypt would be able to cut off the Jewish state's navigation rights through Suez. If the Jews could build their own canal to the Gulf of Aqaba, Weizmann continued, their commerce could slip into the Persian Gulf without having to rely on the Suez Canal. Truman listened carefully to his guest.

In his memoirs, Weizmann attributed the reversal of the United States delegation at the United Nations to the president's direct intervention. In a telephone call later the same afternoon to his representatives at Lake Success, Truman said he believed that Jewish claims to the Negev were reasonable and that they should be respected by the United States. Within a few hours, the Jewish Agency had been able to convince the president that a Jewish state could not be viable if the Negev was removed from its territory.[11] As a result of having direct access to the president, the agency was able to quash attempts to slice away a large part of the proposed Jewish state by effecting a change in American policy. The solution arrived at called for the assignment of the bulk of the Negev to the Jewish state, Aqaba to Jordan, and access to the Gulf of Aqaba to the Jewish state.

At the same time that the Jewish Agency was campaigning in behalf of retaining the Negev for the Jewish state, the Ad Hoc Committee on the Palestine Question was continuing to debate the alternative proposals outlined in UNSCOP's report. On November 25, the committee endorsed the partition, or majority, proposal by a 25–13 vote. Since the General Assembly could not enforce its recommendations, the committee

added an amendment to the plan that requested the Security
Council to take "the necessary measures" to carry out partition.[12] The committee sent the partition plan on to the General Assembly, where a two-thirds vote would be necessary for
adoption. An assembly ballot with the same 25–13 tally as
the one in committee would have defeated the proposal by a
single vote.

THE ARAB RESPONSE TO ZIONISM

Delegates from the Arab states arrived at Lake Success determined to defeat any proposal that would deprive Palestinian Arabs of the right to establish an independent Arab
state throughout all of Palestine. An attempt by the United
Nations to create a Jewish state in the Middle East was
viewed as one more example of the victimization of a segment
of the Arab population to serve the needs of the major powers. The Arab argument was that the major powers should
share responsibility for absorbing the homeless Jewish refugees rather than foisting them on the reluctant Palestinians. A
brief summary of the Arab position is in order before initiat-
ing any discussion of the specific campaign the Arab delegates
undertook in the fall of 1947.

A primary argument against the Jewish plan for Palestine
was that an elemental right of any people is self-determination. Palestine's future must be determined by the country's
indigenous population, which was overwhelmingly non-Jewish. There could be no moral justification, Arabs argued, for
Zionist intentions to establish a Jewish state in a land where
Arabs comprised two-thirds of the population. The United
Nations Special Committee on Palestine estimated that as of
1947 there were 1,203,000 Arabs and 608,000 Jews in Palestine.[13]

Arab leaders were convinced that valid diplomatic promises
made to them concerning Palestine were never honored. Con-

versely, it was believed that other international agreements dealing with Palestine were illegal. From the Arab point of view, this record of diplomatic treachery began with the start of World War I. When the Ottoman Empire sided with the Central Powers, Arab nationalists saw an opportunity to end Turkish rule and acquire independence by joining the Allied cause. Agreement with the British was reached when Sharif Hussein of the Hijaz, an Arab spokesman, and Sir Henry McMahon, British high commissioner of Egypt, exchanged a series of letters that set the terms of the alliance. Arab aid against Turkey was pledged in return for Great Britain's promise to support "the independence of the Arabs in all the regions lying within the frontiers proposed by the Sharif" with certain exceptions. According to the Arab interpretation of the agreement, none of the exceptions included Palestine.[14]

In keeping with this agreement, the successful Arab revolt of 1916 was launched. Meanwhile the British ignored McMahon's commitments to Hussein by entering with the French into the secret Sykes-Picot Agreement of the same year. This latter document parceled out many Arab territories into French- and British-administered zones. According to this division, Palestine was to be internationalized following the war. Chances for an independent Arab Palestine were further clouded when Britain insisted that Palestine was never intended to be included within the area marked for independence by the Hussein-McMahon letters. Although Arab leaders had previously stated that they interpreted the Hussein-McMahon correspondence to include Palestine, Britain had never refuted these announcements. Arab nationalists were convinced that Great Britain was attempting to renege on her original commitment.[15]

Britain's announcement of the Balfour Declaration marked another setback to the cause of an Arab-controlled Palestine. Since the declaration violated the Arab nationalists' interpretation of what they regarded as the legally binding Hussein-McMahon letters, they argued that Balfour's pledge

was illegal.[16] Even had the formal agreement of the
Hussein-McMahon correspondence not existed, these Arabs
believed that the Balfour Declaration was null and void because Palestine was not British and therefore not subject to
British disposition. The Arab leadership opened itself to a
charge of inconsistency by this stand. Britain's right to decide
Palestine's future through the Balfour Declaration was boldly
denied, yet the Arabs had not previously challenged Great
Britain's right to dipose of Palestine according to the agreement reached in the Hussein-McMahon letters. It was further
said that Britain's postwar Mandate for Palestine, which included the exact language of the Balfour Declaration, was in-
valid since it was contrary to the Covenant of the League of
Nations. Inclusion of the declaration, which pledged "the establishment in Palestine of a National Home for the Jewish
people," was viewed as violating the covenant's basic principle
of self-determination.[17]

Opponents of Zionism were encouraged when the report of
the fact-finding King-Crane Commission was published in
1922. The commission was initiated in 1919 when President
Wilson sent, with the approval of the Supreme Council at the
Paris Peace Conference, an American delegation to report on
the situation in the Middle East.[18] This commission, headed
by Dr. Henry King and Charles Crane, recommended to the
peace conference that the Zionist program for Palestine be rejected by the Supreme Council. To ignore the emphatic opposition of the non-Jewish majority—nine-tenths of the total
population—would constitute a flagrant violation of the principle of self-determination. Zionist claims to a "right" to Palestine, the commission concluded, "can hardly be seriously
considered." [19]

From the time Wilson had first announced his Fourteen
Points, which received extensive publicity in the Middle East,
Arabs had emphasized the applicability of the self-determination clause to the Palestine question. The King-Crane Commission, by endorsing the primacy of self-determination, rein-

forced the Arab argument. Publication of the report in 1922 encouraged the Arabs to believe that eventually their cause would win the international support that would be needed to blunt the Zionist drive for Palestine.[20] By September 1947, however, Zionism had clearly gained ground in its effort to create a Jewish state in Palestine. Arab delegates at Lake Success realized that they would have difficulty in attempting to defeat the partition resolution. Events in Europe during the Second World War had awakened sympathy throughout the world for Jewish statehood. It was the contention of Arab spokesmen that additional support for Zionism arose from national leaders who believed that establishing a Jewish state in Palestine would remove the possibility that Jewish refugees would have to be absorbed by their own countries. Although international support for a Jewish state was at high tide when the General Assembly session began, the Arab delegations were not without their resources.

As mentioned previously in this chapter, the bloc of Arab states had successfully combined with the Latin American bloc in the United Nations to elect all their candidates to the Economic and Social Council. This combination was also utilized to obtain Syria's defeat of India in an election for a Security Council seat. If the six Arab and twenty Latin American countries voted as a bloc on the partition proposal, it would guarantee the measure's defeat. Thomas Hamilton, the *New York Times* correspondent at the United Nations, reported that such a coalition was indeed possible.[21] Widespread defection among Latin American delegations was, however, to prove costly to the Arab side.[22]

Arab representatives actively canvassed for votes among the other delegates.[23] A small Arab victory was attained when the port of Jaffa, which had been assigned to the Jewish state under partition, was relocated within the Arab state. Since Jaffa's population was estimated to be 90 percent Arab, even the Jewish Agency endorsed this boundary change.[24] But Arab victories at the fall meeting were few. Arab delegates did not lose their battle by default; a vigorous lobbying campaign took place until the final vote was under way. Representatives of the Arab case at Lake Success were overwhelmed by what proved to be a far more sophisticated and better-planned campaign carried on by the Jewish Agency.

THE STRUGGLE FOR VOTES

With the potential existence of a Jewish state hanging in the balance, the Zionists intensified their lobbying. It was an emotional time for Zionism's supporters, both Jew and non-Jew, who believed that the Jewish people of the world would be safe only when a Jewish state existed. The events of the next few weeks were viewed as being crucial to any hopes of statehood. Jewish Agency representatives at Lake Success mobilized American Jewry for an extraordinary effort. One member of the agency's United Nations delegation, David Horowitz, remarked that the native Jewish community "flung itself into the thick of the fray with an enthusiasm and dedication which had no parallel or standard of comparison in all past experience." According to Horowitz, not one influential Jew refused a call to help secure the needed votes.[25] Prominent Jews were asked to exert pressure and make appeals all over the world. Bernard Baruch, who insisted he had no commitment to Zionism, was disheartened by this activity. In a draft of a telegram to a friend, Herbert Bayard Swope, Baruch wrote that he "went along" with Zionist requests, but "the whole thing makes me sick." [26] Sol Bloom of New York, an influential Jewish member of the House of Representatives, revealed his contribution: "In my own humble way I approached the representatives of several countries, including the Philippines, Haiti, Liberia, and others, and in most instances I was successful in obtaining their support [for partition] and in one or two cases their abstention rather than casting a negative vote." [27]

Non-Jews also participated in the agency's effort to win votes. United States Senator Robert Wagner, United Nations Secretary-General Trygve Lie, General Assembly President Oswaldo Aranha, and Guatemala's representative to the United Nations, Jorge García-Granados, all worked to secure passage of the partition plan.[28]

Truman's role during the final days preceding General Assembly passage of the partition scheme has been a source of controversy. Some reports have charged the president with exerting coercion on wavering nations. Sumner Welles, for example, has written that by "direct order of the White House every form of pressure, direct and indirect, was brought to bear by American officials upon those countries . . . that were known to be either uncertain or opposed to partition." [29] Truman was urged to take such a direction by the Zionists and their supporters. Congressman Celler suggested, for example, that the president put pressure on nations that were hostile to partition. Celler pointed out that Greece, "which is immeasurably and morally indebted to us, . . . and other countries friendly with us [should be informed] that we expect their cooperation on the matter of Palestine." [30] The chairman of the Executive Committee of the American Jewish Conference, Louis Lipsky, similarly pleaded with the chief executive to help line up the needed votes.[31] Evidence indicates that Truman responded in a very limited way until shortly before the final vote on partition in the General Assembly. He was aware of the "constant barrage" of appeals for presidential action. "I do not think," he recalled, "I ever had as much pressure and propaganda aimed at the White House as I had in this instance." As he had done before, Truman displayed his anger at some "Zionist leaders . . . engaging in political threats." [32]

Members of the United States delegation at the United Nations had made no effort to influence other nations' votes on the Palestine issue until a few days before the balloting. Thomas Hamilton of the *New York Times* reported on November 27—just two days before the assembly vote—that the "partition vote has little chance unless the United States makes strenuous efforts to win over some delegations that otherwise have sided with the United States" on major issues.[33] An urgent message received by the president on the same day —November 27—indicated that the American delegation had not been attempting to obtain votes for partition from other countries. Judge Joseph M. Proskauer, president of the American Jewish Committee, followed up a meeting he had recently held with Truman by sending a telegram which said in part that in his opinion "a dangerous situation has been created by various alleged expressions that our delegation was directed not to use affirmative persuasion on other delegations to vote for partition." He closed by urging that the United States position shift from one of passive to one of active support of the partition proposal.[34] Apparently just a short time before Proskauer sent his telegram, the instructions to the American delegates at the United Nations changed. Although the role played by the American delegation was a limited one, it should be noted that the White House did respond to pressure from Zionists and act in their behalf at United Nations headquarters.

During the final days before the General Assembly vote, the American delegation actively solicited the votes of other countries in support of the partition plan. The preponderance of evidence strongly indicates that the change was ordered by the president. No record of Truman's order is to be found in his papers at the Truman Library. However, those who participated in the battle at Lake Success have said that they were aware that the order for the United States delegation to switch from passive to active support came from the White House. According to the Jewish Agency's David Horowitz, the instructions came directly from Truman. "America's line of action had swung in a new direction," Horowitz later wrote. "As a result of instructions from the President, the State Department now embarked on a helpful course of great importance to our own interest." [35]

Jewish Congressman Emanuel Celler's correspondence with Truman is perhaps more revealing. Celler, who was extremely close to the Zionist leadership, informed Truman in a November 26 telegram that he had "spent considerable time at Lake Success" during the campaign for partition. Celler added that he was

> seriously disturbed that the vote for partition . . . may fail by one or two votes. Thus all your excellent efforts will be frustrated at the eleventh hour. Apparently our delegates are under instruction to conduct conversations only in a limited way with delegations of recalcitrant countries like Greece that are abstaining or voting against partition. . . . May I respectfully request that our delegation throw off some of its restraint in its conversations with Greece and other countries friendly with us and indicate that we expect cooperation on the matter of partition.[36]

On December 3, 1947, several days after the partition resolution had been approved, Celler wrote a "personal and confidential" letter to Truman. Celler offered his "sincerest gratitude for the effective work you did" in actively assisting the passage of partition.[37] Another letter written by Celler the same day indicates that perhaps Matthew Connelly, secretary to the president, might have had something to do with passing Truman's order on to the American delegation. Celler thanked Connelly for "the very effective work you did in bringing about the desired result in the voting on the Palestine Resolution." [38] Congressman Arthur G. Klein, another representative with close ties to the Zionist leaders, said on December 2, 1947, that "there can be no doubt that the successful fight of the American delegation was made at the personal direction of President Truman." [39]

Despite its more active role just prior to the final vote, the United States delegation used its influence on behalf of the partition plan to a very limited extent. One member of the group wrote that the delegates "tried as best we could to per-

suade other countries" of the necessity for partition, but that
they never resorted to threats or intimidation.[40] García-Granados, a close ally of the Jewish Agency's delegation at Lake
Success, has emphasized how mild the American effort was:
"At no time did their campaign go over the heads of the delegates to the various governments involved." [41] Another Latin
American diplomat who was present at the time of the vote
agrees: "There was only a presentation of United States views.
Even this was not very strong." [42]

Although restrained, the American contribution was considered by some participants in the struggle for passage to be
a significant one. David Horowitz of the Jewish Agency
argued that the "firmer and more active line" taken by the
United States was extremely useful in capturing the votes of
some wavering nations. Horowitz noted of the American role:

> The improved atmosphere [created by America's active sup-
> port] swayed a number of wavering countries. The United
> States exerted the weight of its influence almost at the last
> hour, and *the way the final vote turned out must be ascribed
> to this fact.* Its [the American] intervention sidetracked the
> manipulation of the "fringe votes" against us.[43]

Harry L. Shapiro, the executive director of the American Zionist Emergency Council, said that the activity of the American delegation "unquestionably was the major factor in this
historic decision" by the United Nations to create a Jewish
state by passing the partition plan.[44]

Because the limited amount of American intervention did
prove to be of influence, many observers overlooked the fact
that Truman had used almost none of the power at his command to secure votes. David Niles's activities during this period give an indication of the nature of the president's commitment. A few days prior to the General Assembly balloting, the administrative assistant telephoned a prominent
Greek-American businessman and asked him to cable the

Greek government recommending a vote in favor of partition.[45] Had the White House been interested in pressuring Greece into supporting the plan, a more direct and effective manner would have been employed.[46] In 1947 the Greek government was relying on massive assistance from the United States in order to counter communist strength within the country. In the absence of overt American pressure, however, the explanation for the Greek votes most likely rests on pressures which have yet to be uncovered by researchers.

THE GENERAL ASSEMBLY APPROVES PARTITION

In the interval between the Ad Hoc Committee vote on November 25, 1947, and the official General Assembly balloting on November 29, the Zionists were able to turn an impending defeat into a triumph. As late as one day before the vote, the outcome was still very much in doubt. Oswaldo Aranha, the president of the General Assembly, reflected the doubt that prevailed at United Nations headquarters. During the morning of November 28—a day before the final balloting—Aranha said he thought that partition would lose. A few hours later, at the lunch recess, Aranha reversed himself and reported that he believed partition would pass after all.[47]

Late in the afternoon of November 29, 1947, the United Nations General Assembly passed the partition plan by a vote of 33–13.[48] A negative switch of three votes would have changed the outcome to 30–16, or one less than the necessary two-thirds. A number of sources of influence, as well as a mass of conflicting evidence, makes it difficult to determine the exact manner in which the needed votes were secured. Relying on the continued assistance of its allies, the Jewish Agency chose its final targets with care. Haiti, Liberia, and the Philippines, none of which had supported partition in the committee vote on November 25, 1947, each cast a favorable ballot four days later.[49] It is unclear what occurred during the final days to win over the votes of these nations.[50]

THE STRUGGLE FOR PRESIDENTIAL FAVOR

During the fall of 1947 the opposing camps in Washington waged a spirited contest to win the president's support for their respective proposals for Palestine policy. Members of the administration who called for greater support of the Zionists were the most conspicuous. Following Truman's Yom Kippur statement in 1946, the Democratic National Committee received large amounts of money from grateful Jewish contributors.[51] At the conclusion of a cabinet meeting on September 4, 1947, Postmaster-General Robert Hannegan told the president that another statement favorable to the Jews would be of great assistance to the committee in raising needed campaign funds for the following year.[52] During another cabinet meeting one month later, on October 6, 1947, Hannegan commented that some of the party's most important past contributors wanted assurances from the administration of its support for the Jewish claims in Palestine. According to Secretary of Defense James Forrestal, Truman refused to commit himself to such an approach at that time.[53]

J. Howard McGrath, chairman of the Democratic National Committee, told Forrestal that two or three pivotal states could be lost in the 1948 election unless Truman backed the Zionist demands.[54] Niles continued to encourage the president to increase his friendship with the Zionists.[55] Once the Jewish Agency approved the partition plan, prominent Democrats urged Truman to give the proposal American support.[56] In one of these appeals, Robert Wagner asked the president not to be swayed by the pressure that the Arabs would bring to bear on him.[57] Truman, who was annoyed by the incessant Zionist efforts to obtain his endorsement, bluntly replied to Wagner: "I know of no pressure except the pressure of the Jews, which has always been extensive and continuous."[58]

7

The American Reversal

THE ZIONIST CAMPAIGN FOR SUPPORT OF IMPLEMENTATION OF PARTITION

Spokesmen for the United States urged that the United Nations fully implement its decision for partition without any hesitation. American delegate Herschel Johnson stated his government's belief that "the threat or use of force" in opposition to a United Nations decision could not be tolerated, even if it were necessary to mobilize and use a volunteer United Nations constabulary.[1] One reason for this unequivocal stand was a firm belief in Washington that London, despite statements that indicated the opposite, would cooperate in the implementation.[2] Secretary-General Trygve Lie noted that "most countries expected Britain as the original sponsor of United Nations action to do its utmost toward carrying the action through."[3]

In the weeks following the adoption of partition, London, eager to limit its obligations, made it clear that the British government would accept the partition decision, but not cooperate by implementing it, since implementation might require the use of armed forces. Until the expiration of the Mandate on May 15, 1948, the British would rule Palestine, but following that date they would leave immediately.[4]

American support for partition, as well as the government's initial call for swift implementation, put Truman back in favor with the Zionists for the time being. Even during the days of celebration that followed the United Nations resolution of November 29, 1947, however, supporters of the establishment of a Jewish state were warned that they "must not let down now." [5] By early 1948 the Zionists had ample evidence to justify their concern. Not only had British refusal to cooperate complicated United Nations plans for implementation, but increasingly strained relations between the United States and the Soviet Union worked against the Zionists. Genuine alarm swept through Washington in February 1948 as the Kremlin carried out a Communist coup in Czechoslovakia. In particular, the suspicious circumstances surrounding the death of the popular Czech foreign minister, Jan Masaryk, added to the distrust between Russia and America. Although the Soviets insisted Masaryk's death was a suicide, the evidence strongly suggested foul play. Washington was also worried about the approaching 1948 election in Italy, for it appeared that the large Communist party there would receive enough votes to win. Concerned that a Communist government would move Italy into the Soviet camp, the United States dramatically increased its aid to Italy in an effort to blunt the Communist party's ability to profit from the economic dislocations resulting from the war. With Czechoslovakia and Italy providing the settings for two looming international crises, the Jews braced for a battle against those Washington opponents who argued that the time was wrong for any showdown in Palestine.[6]

Chaim Weizmann had gone to London after the partition vote in the United Nations. In mid-January 1948, the Jewish Agency persuaded him to return to America and "co-operate with it in the gathering crisis." [7] Since Weizmann had developed a cordial relationship with the president, the Zionists hoped that the Jewish leader could use his influence to convince Truman to stand behind the policy of allegiance to United Nations implementation.[8]

In addition, friendly congressmen who backed the Jewish effort in Palestine urged Truman to remain firm on the question of implementation.[9] Newspaper advertisements and public rallies were employed to keep the issue before the public.[10] Fifteen thousand persons participated in one parade and outdoor rally in New York City in spite of a driving rain that at one point changed to a "hail of ice the size of pebbles." [11] Truman was annoyed by the increased pressure. Writing to one Jewish leader, the president made clear how displeased he was with much of the lobbying:

> One of our principal difficulties in getting the Palestine matter settled . . . has been that there are so many people in this country who know more about how the situation can be handled than do those in authority. It has made the situation exceedingly difficult and is not contributing in any manner to its solution. . . . [T]he matter is now in the hands of the United Nations and the United States is making every effort to maintain the position of the United Nations Commission [established to implement partition]. So much lobbying and outside interference has been going on in this question that it is almost impossible to get a fair-minded approach to the subject.[12]

When he wrote his *Memoirs,* the president recalled the manner in which some of the Zionists approached him:

> The Jewish pressure on the White House did not diminish in the days following the partition vote in the U.N. Individuals and groups asked me, usually in rather quarrelsome and emotional ways, to stop the Arabs, to keep the British from supporting the Arabs, to furnish American soldiers, to do this, that, and the other. I think I can say that I kept my faith in the rightness of my policy in spite of some of the Jews. When I say "the Jews," I mean, of course, the extreme Zionists. I know that most Americans of Jewish faith, while they hoped for the restoration of [the] Jewish homeland, are and always have been Americans first and foremost.
>
> As the pressure mounted, I found it necessary to give instructions that I did not want to be approached by any more spokesmen for the extreme Zionist cause. I was even so dis-

turbed that I put off seeing Dr. Chaim Weizmann, who had returned to the United States and had asked for an interview with me.[13]

Concerned that Washington was reappraising its Palestine position, the Zionists wanted to obtain a White House interview for Weizmann. The persuasive Jewish leader appeared to be the ideal person to explain why the Zionists believed it was so important that Truman stand behind the American policy of implementation without delay. When Weizmann asked to see the president, however, he was thwarted by the policy that excluded Zionist spokesmen. The White House replied that seeing Truman was "out of the question." [14]

Masterfully using their available resources, the Zionists were able to circumvent the presidential edict. With the disappointed Weizmann lying ill in his hotel, his friend Frank Goldman, the president of B'nai B'rith, telephoned Edward "Eddie" Jacobson in Kansas City. Jacobson, a Jew who was one of the president's closest personal friends, and a partner in their ill-fated haberdashery, was informed that the political leaders of New York City, including Edward Flynn, had been unable to obtain an entry into the White House for Weizmann. Goldman added that Truman was bitter as a result of the conduct and discourtesies of some Zionist leaders. Since all else had failed, Jacobson was asked to get in touch with the president personally and beg him to see Weizmann.[15]

Jacobson sent a telegram to the White House the following day, February 21, 1948. His message, which sympathized with the pressure the president faced, included a personal appeal to Truman: "I have asked you for very little in the way of favors during all our years of friendship, but am begging of you to see Dr. Weizmann. . . ." [16] When Truman refused, Jacobson went to Washington and arranged to speak with the president on March 13, 1948. Matthew Connelly, the secretary to the president, "begged Jacobson not to discuss Palestine with the President." That subject, of course, was the very reason for Jacobson's visit to the White House. When Jacobson raised the issue of Palestine, he recalled, Truman "immediately became tense in appearance, abrupt in speech and very bitter. . . . In all the years of our friendship he [Truman] never talked to me in this manner. . . ." Jacobson then told the president that Weizmann, "an old and a sick man, had made his long journey to the United States especially to see Truman." The president replied by commenting on "how disrespectful and how mean" some of the Jewish spokesmen had been. "I suddenly found myself thinking," Jacobson later wrote, "that my dear friend, the President of the United States, was at that moment as close to being an anti-Semite as a man could possibly be." Sensing that his mission had failed, and finding himself unable "to soften [Truman's] anger," Jacobson noticed a small statue of Andrew Jackson in the president's office. Suddenly emboldened, Jacobson remarked that he knew of Truman's admiration for Jackson; he then said, "Well, Harry, I too have a hero [Weizmann] . . . the greatest Jew who ever lived." It was unfair to refuse to see Weizmann, Jacobson bluntly continued, "because you were insulted by some of our American Jewish leaders. . . . It does not sound like you, Harry, because I thought that you could take this stuff they have been handing out to you." Truman, in his huge swivel chair, abruptly spun himself away from Jacobson. For a moment the president stared out the window toward the rose garden, then spun himself back around and said: "You win, you baldheaded [son of a bitch]. I will see him." [17]

The president agreed to see Weizmann, but only on an off-the-record basis. Traveling to Washington incognito, the Jewish leader entered the White House grounds unnoticed through the East Gate on March 18, 1948. During an extremely cordial session, Truman assured his guest that he was concerned with the well-being of the Jewish people. Although Weizmann had asked for only twenty-five minutes, Truman extended the interview another twenty minutes. One reason why Jacobson did not accompany Weizmann to the White House was that it was

believed that he should be "saved" in case he was needed for
another emergency. Weizmann told Jacobson, "You have a job
to do so keep the White House doors open." [18] Jacobson had
an easy time getting around White House protocol. When he
called for an appointment with the president, he was usually
told to come right over. [19]

LEO ISACSON'S ELECTION
STUNS THE DEMOCRATS

At about the same time that Jacobson arranged for Weizmann's meeting with Truman, it became apparent that Jewish
voters who were dissatisfied with the president's Palestine policy might well decide to withhold their votes from Democrats.
Democratic party professionals wrote to Truman early in
1948 and suggested that a pro-Jewish policy in the Middle
East would brighten the domestic political situation. Party
leaders in New York State expressed concern over Palestine's
potential for becoming an explosive political issue in 1948.
New York City Congressman Andrew L. Somers asked Truman if a delegation could present the president with a petition
bearing 35,000 signatures in behalf of an American policy favorable to Zionism. According to the memorandum which
summarized Somer's telephone call, "he thinks it would be
wise, politically, for the President to receive them." [20] Former
New Jersey governor A. Harry Moore informed Truman how
important the Jewish vote was in New Jersey for a statewide
candidate. [21] Some public opinion mail warned the president
along similar lines. For example, one writer pointed out:
"Jews who vote Democratic ticket expect your immediate in-
tercession in Palestine." [22] *New York Times* writer Warren
Moscow reported that New York City Democratic leader Edward Flynn informed Truman of grave political consequences
should the president not fully endorse the Jewish program for

Palestine.[23] Any widespread alienation of the Jewish voters could finish Democratic aspirations to carry the state, since 47 percent of the country's Jews lived there, and approximately 17 percent of the state's voters were Jewish.

Discontent stemmed in large measure from a decision made by the State Department. On December 5, 1947, less than one week after United Nations adoption of partition, Secretary of State George C. Marshall announced that as a result of growing violence there, the State Department was imposing an embargo on all shipments of arms to the Middle East. Since both the Arabs and the Jews were already well supplied with arms, the embargo did not appreciably improve the chances for a peaceful settlement. Although the State Department insisted that its action in this instance was consistent with long-established policies, it appeared to many Jews to be a significant retreat from America's support of partition. The embargo was viewed by its critics as being a part of the more serious failure of the Truman administration to work actively for implementing the partition plan in the Middle East. Since the Jews had declared their willingness to accept United Nations implementation and the Arabs had vowed to fight it, it seemed to much of the Jewish community to be clearly unfair to treat both sides alike.[24]

In the 1948 presidential election, New York, with its forty-seven electoral votes, would clearly be the most important state for any candidate to win. Democratic hopes of capturing the state in 1948 had been dimmed by the presidential candidacy of former vice president Henry Wallace. Campaigning on a progressive program that was to the political left of Truman's policies, Wallace had won the endorsement of the American Labor party. This party, which emerged during the 1930s, was a union-based political organization in New York that sponsored liberal candidates. In 1944, when the ALP backed the Democratic candidate Franklin D. Roosevelt, 496,405 New Yorkers cast their ballots for the incumbent

president on the "ALP line." Roosevelt won New York's electoral votes, but only as a result of the half-million votes he received as the ALP candidate.[25]

With no prospect of gaining the significant sponsorship of
the ALP, it became extremely important to Truman that he
satisfy New York's large Jewish community, which could normally be counted on to support Democratic candidates for
president. Results of a congressional by-election on February
17, 1948, indicated, however, that Truman's Palestine policy
was alienating Jewish voters. A special election in the Bronx
was expected to be won by Karl Propper, a candidate of Edward Flynn's regular Democratic organization. However, Leo
Isacson, the candidate of the ALP and Wallace, "scored a
sweeping and surprising victory," rolling up an impressive
55.8 percent of the vote as opposed to Propper's 31 percent.
New York Times political reporter Warren Moscow wrote that
in political circles Isacson "never had been considered to have
a chance to win." [26]

Isacson's victory in a district in which Jewish voters comprised 55 percent of the electorate was credited to the "militantly pro-Palestine appeal made by Mr. Isacson, Wallace, and
other supporters." [27] Wallace, who spent considerable time in
the district on behalf of Isacson, scored Truman for his failure
to promote United Nations implementation of partition. According to Wallace, Truman "still talks Jewish but acts
Arab." [28]

Propper's defeat in a usually safe Democratic district "unquestionably reflected dissatisfaction with the present United
States attitude on implementing the Palestine partition"
plan.[29] Propper, who strongly endorsed the Zionist program,
had specifically called for the establishment of a United Nations force to insure that partition would be enforced immediately and effectively. Jewish voters, however, rejected the
Democratic candidate largely because the Democratic administration in Washington was not working hard enough for
United States implementation of partition. Veteran political

observer James A. Hagerty noted that in the wake of the balloting, "a political realization is that Truman had little, if any, chance of winning" New York State in the fall of 1948.[30]

New York Democrats, led by Flynn, lost no time in expressing to Truman their displeasure with his handling of the Palestine issue. In order to avert a Democratic disaster that could bury the party's entire slate of candidates along with the president, Truman was urged to sponsor the establishment of a United Nations police force, if necessary, to enforce partition. Three days after the special congressional election, the *New York Times* reported, high-ranking New York State Democrats used a Jefferson-Jackson Day dinner to urge Truman to lift the arms embargo and work for the policy that had been so strongly endorsed by Isacson and Wallace—the establishment of a United Nations police force to implement the partition plan. *Times* writer Clayton Knowles noted that three prominent New York State Democrats—Flynn, State Chairman Paul E. Fitzpatrick, and Franklin D. Roosevelt, Jr.— had personally contacted the president and informed him of their concern.[31] The criticism aimed at Truman came from sources other than New York State's Democrats. For example, writing on behalf of a group of the state's Liberal party voters who had been supporting Truman instead of Wallace because of the former's stronger stand against communism, X. Farbman warned: "We cannot support Wallace . . . but we'll be equally vehement against your administration if pattern of good words and no action continues on Palestine and other issues." [32]

TRUMAN ADVISED TO OPPOSE
IMPLEMENTATION OF PARTITION

Arab threats to oppose implementation with arms "to the last man," coupled with Britain's flat refusal to involve herself with the settlement, served as a signal that a United Nations

constabulary would have to be mobilized to enforce partition.[33] Secretary-General Lie argued that the United Nations
had no choice but to implement its Palestine decision, however high the cost. To back away from threatened violence,
Lie stressed, "will lessen the prestige of the United Nations,
and confidence in it will be reduced." [34]

In spite of Truman's public assurances that he would not
send American troops into Palestine, some high-ranking administration officials insisted that the United States would be
under strong pressure to supply men for an international
peace force. During a briefing, on February 18, 1948, on the
nation's available military strength, General Alfred Gruenther
explained to the president the difficulties of committing any
armed force.[35] United States military strategists estimated that
a forcible application of partition would take anywhere from
80,000 to 160,000 troops. America was not in a position to
supply even a small share of the needed men, Gruenther
pointed out, since any request for more than a division (approximately 15,000 troops) could be met only by partial mobilization.[36]

As part of their offensive against the implementation of
partition, the Arab governments threatened to reconsider
American oil concessions unless the Truman administration
adopted a more sympathetic position.[37] In Syria, for example,
the Parliament refused to ratify an agreement concerning
transit rights for a proposed oil pipeline, to be sponsored by
American companies, from the Persian Gulf to the Mediterranean.[38] In February 1948 the Arab League recommended to
its member states that they stop United States interests from
laying any pipelines pending a more favorable Washington policy.[39] Secretary of Defense Forrestal was disturbed by the
Arab activities. Fearful of an eventual serious shortage of petroleum, he predicted that "American motorcar companies
would have to design a four-cylinder motorcar sometime
within the next five years." [40] Forrestal repeatedly warned
Truman of the dangers involved should the hostile Arab gov-

ernments cut off American access to Middle Eastern oil.[41]

State Department and military advisers argued that by antagonizing the Arabs the administration was risking their shift into the Soviet camp. The strategic considerations involved in such a loss concerned the military planners.[42] Dean Rusk, director of the State Department's Office of Special Political Affairs, cautioned that the Soviets were likely to try to gain control in Palestine by capitalizing on the widespread violence that would follow Britain's withdrawal. In order to block a Soviet move, Rusk said, the United States would feel impelled to intervene as part of a United Nations force, yet American troops were not available for such a move.[43]

Anxious to remove the influence of domestic politics from determining Palestine policy, Forrestal urged the leaders of both political parties to adopt a bipartisan, nonpolitical approach to the issue. He learned from Republican Senator Arthur Vandenberg that "there was a feeling among most Republicans that the Democratic party had used the Palestine question politically, and the Republicans felt they were entitled to make similar use of the issue." [44] Forrestal discovered that the leaders in each party, including Truman and Governor Dewey, were skeptical of entering into any informal agreement. Unable to obtain satisfactory results, the secretary of defense abandoned his efforts to secure a bipartisan policy in February 1948.[45]

Forrestal did continue to work within the administration for a policy opposing implementation of partition. On January 21, 1948, Undersecretary of State Robert Lovett showed Forrestal a memorandum that the State Department Planning Staff had just completed. The document stated that any American commitment to support implementation was based on the assumption that application of the plan could be carried out without force. Since the plan for peaceful implementation was unworkable, the Planning Staff recommended that the United States delegation propose that the United Nations withdraw its partition plan. A week later Forrestal, Dean

Rusk, and Loy Henderson (director of the State Department's Office of Near Eastern and African Affairs) gathered to discuss America's Palestine policy. Henderson agreed with Forrestal that enough evidence was available "to support a statement that unworkability of the proposed solution would justify a re-examination." [46]

On February 12, 1948, Truman's refusal to discuss the Palestine issue with the press indicated that the future direction of American policy was under examination.[47] The same day, during a meeting of the National Security Council, Secretary of State Marshall spoke of a memorandum he had just received. Prepared by the State Department, the document outlined three alternative directions for the Palestine policy of the United States. The three proposals were: (1) direct abandonment of the partition plan, (2) vigorous support for implementation of partition, forcibly if necessary, and (3) a request that the whole Palestine question be referred back to the General Assembly for review. None of the three approaches had yet received Marshall's endorsement.[48]

A REVERSAL OF
AMERICA'S PALESTINE POLICY

When the General Assembly adopted partition on November 29, 1947, the resolution created a United Nations Palestine Commission that was charged with the task of implementing the decision.[49] The commission's hopes of organizing a peaceful transfer of administrative responsibility from the mandatory power to the two new states soon vanished. Representing Palestine's Arab community, the Arab Higher Committee notified the Palestine Commission that it would not cooperate at all. The commission then "was informed [by Britain] that it was not [her] intention . . . to facilitate in any way the implementation" of partition. London flatly refused the commission's request for a progressive transfer of authority. All control would be transferred on May 15, 1948, the British made clear, and none before that date.[50]

Unable to cope with Arab intransigence and British passivity, the Palestine Commission bluntly reported to the United Nations Security Council, on February 16, 1948, that unless it received "military forces in adequate strength," it would be unable to implement partition. Accusing the Arabs "both inside and outside Palestine" of a "deliberate effort to alter [the partition plan] by force," the commission report warned that unless the Security Council acted, May 15 would initiate "a period of uncontrolled, widespread strife and bloodshed."[51]

American representatives did not respond immediately to the Palestine Commission's call for an international constabulary. Warren Austin, the United States ambassador to the United Nations, proposed on February 24, 1948, that a special Security Council committee further investigate whether the Palestine situation represented a threat to peace.[52] A member of the Soviet delegation, correctly sensing that American policy was in a state of flux, commented: "Very interesting speech, but precisely what does the United States want?"[53]

At the same time that the Security Council was being asked to create an international police force to impose partition, Truman was engaged in a serious review of his Palestine policy. When he learned of the preparations for war that were going on in the Middle East, the president privately wrote to Arab leaders on February 13, 1948, and appealed for restraint and moderation on their part. The request was flatly rejected by the Arabs.[54] Truman was especially disturbed about the prospect of a civil war in Palestine because a dangerously tense international situation already prevailed. Late in February 1948, worsening East–West relations took an ominous turn when the communists overthrew the government of Czechoslovakia. Facing a possible conflagration in Europe, Truman hoped to forestall the eruption of a major crisis in the Middle East. He feared that the United States would be required to respond with troops should total war break out in Palestine. If American troops were tied down in Palestine, Truman would have less military leverage in Europe.[55]

Increasing international tension made proposals to postpone a Palestine showdown more appealing. One week after the Czechoslovak coup d'état, a top-secret telegram was received in Washington from General Lucius Clay in Berlin. Clay ominously warned:

> For many months . . . I have felt and held that war was unlikely for at least ten years. Within the last few weeks, I have felt a subtle change in Soviet attitude which I cannot define but which now gives me a feeling that it [war] may come with dramatic suddenness. . . .[56]

At about the same time that he learned of Clay's prediction, Truman made a decision to accept the advice of his State Department counselors with regard to Palestine. The department's recommendations were included in a memorandum prepared for the president by Henderson, Lovett, and Rusk. The document argued that any attempt to carry out partition, with the ensuing risk of involvement in a war against the Arabs, was antagonistic to the national security of the United States. Truman, who agreed that the current international situation made a change of direction for American policy necessary, approved sometime before March 8, 1948, a State Department draft of a statement to be read at the United Nations. This draft called on the United Nations to set its partition decision aside and install a temporary United Nations trusteeship in Palestine.

Included among the Clark Clifford Papers at the Truman Library in Independence, Missouri, is a memorandum which makes it possible to trace with certainty the events concerning the American reversal. Written in Clifford's own hand, this undated, untitled two-page memorandum was prepared shortly after the reversal. It reveals that on March 8, 1948, Marshall informed Ambassador Austin that Truman had approved the draft.[57]

Also on March 8, the president discussed the Palestine situation with officials of the Democratic National Committee. "We have the Zionist Jews in the office every day," Jack Redding, the committee's publicity director, told Truman, "and the pressure is building up a terrific head of steam." By this time Truman had made his as yet unannounced decision to accept State Department advice, regardless of the political repercussions. "It's no use putting pressure on the Committee," Truman said. "The Palestine issue will be handled here. And there'll be no politics involved." [58]

On March 16, Marshall directed Austin to present the new American policy to the United Nations "as soon as possible as Austin believes appropriate." No plans were made to inform the president when Austin was to speak. The exact phrasing of the speech was never submitted to Truman for his approval, but the Clifford memorandum states that the final text included "the same substance" as the initial draft that Truman had endorsed.[59]

Truman conferred with Weizmann on March 18.[60] The next day Austin formally asked the United Nations to postpone, and perhaps eventually abandon, partition.[61] The timing made it appear that Truman, who had been so cordial the previous day, had broken faith with Weizmann. Signals between the State Department and the White House had somehow become crossed. The department assumed that it had discretionary power to announce the policy change without further consultation with the president. Department officials were not aware of the Weizmann–Truman conference. Truman was embarrassed and incensed by the inappropriate timing. He telephoned the State Department, and emphatically said that he should have been told when the speech was going to be delivered.[62]

A myth has existed since the time of the event itself that the State Department acted independently in regard to the reversal. According to this version, Truman, who was not at all responsible, first learned of the American reversal only after Austin had spoken to the United Nations. An account by Jonathan Daniels, for example, is indicative of the explanations of the reversal that have gained wide circulation. Daniels wrote that Truman called Clifford early in the morning the day after Austin's speech, and said: "Can you come right down? There's a story in the papers on Palestine and I don't understand what has happened." Truman, according to Daniels, instructed Clifford "to find out how this could have happened; I assured Chaim Weizmann that we were for partition and would stick to it. He must think that I am a plain liar." [63]

In his *Memoirs*, Truman further clouds the facts concerning the reversal. Referring to "the State Department's trusteeship proposal," he strongly implies that he had nothing to do with the scheme. At one point he argues that "anybody in the State Department should have known . . . that the Jews would read this proposal as a complete abandonment of the partition plan. . . . In this sense, the trusteeship idea was at odds with my attitude and the policy I had laid down." [64]

Both Truman and historians friendly to him have written that the reversal resulted from the independent actions of the State Department. But the truth is that Truman directly and knowingly approved the shift in the Palestine policy of the United States.

8

The American Proposal
for a United Nations Trusteeship

THE FAILURE OF AMERICAN POLICY

On March 19, 1948, United States Ambassador Warren Austin recommended that the United Nations summon "an immediate special session" to reconsider the entire Palestine question. Pending a decision on the permanent status of the Holy Land, Austin continued, the United Nations should administer Palestine by means of a temporary trusteeship. Since the partition proposal "cannot now be implemented" by peaceful means, the United States proposed that the Security Council instruct the Palestine Commission to suspend its efforts in behalf of implementing partition.[1]

As delegates listened unbelievingly to the American abandonment of the partition plan that the United States had helped to pass, "there was pin-drop silence and bewilderment" throughout the hall.[2] Austin said that the proposed trusteeship should be "without prejudice" to the eventual political settlement in Palestine. This new policy was necessitated, he noted, by the Security Council's unwillingness "to go ahead with efforts to implement [the partition] plan in the existing situation."[3] Before any trusteeship could be established, Austin emphasized, the United Nations' immediate task would be to bring about a truce between Jews and Arabs. A virtual state of war, escalating with each passing week, already existed in Palestine.[4] Austin's reasoning was hardly convincing, for it had been the United States that had blocked Security

Council attempts to mobilize an international police force to implement partition.[5]

Secretary of State Marshall informed the president on March 24, 1948, that the State Department was "working on plans for a truce and that it was felt that there was a good possibility that a truce could be effectuated." Truman was also told that the State Department expected to know definitely about chances for a truce by April 7.[6] State Department optimism concerning the possibility of a Palestine truce proved unwarranted. The status of a Jewish state during any armistice was an irreconcilable issue. Jewish leadership flatly rejected any military truce that deferred the establishment of the Jewish commonwealth past May 15, 1948. On April 29, 1948, Moshe Sharett, speaking on behalf of the Jewish Agency for Palestine, officially notified Marshall that the truce as proposed by the United States was unacceptable. "The main objections as I saw them," Sharett wrote,

> were: first, that the proposed truce entails the deferment of statehood and renders its attainment in the future most uncertain, thereby gravely prejudicing our rights and position; second, that as the effective operation of the truce obviously involves the presence and the use in Palestine of a considerable force, we cannot but assume that the intention is to keep the British forces in occupation and control of Palestine. I was also greatly concerned about the gross inequality under which we would be placed as regards arms and military training: the Arab states would be entirely free to acquire arms and stock-pile them for eventual use in Palestine against us; Palestinian and other Arabs would be free to train en masse in any of the neighboring countries; we would be precluded from either acquiring arms or [undertaking] any large scale training—training which we could only organize in Palestine.[7]

"It is the feeling of the Jewish world," remarked Sharett, "that it [the time for a Jewish state] is now or never." [8] It had been extremely difficult to secure the necessary votes for the partition plan the previous fall; the Zionists wanted no part of waging a second campaign to win United Nations approval for a Jewish state. A reversal of the decision on partition because of Arab threats, according to Chaim Weizmann, would be nothing more than "pure appeasement of aggression." [9]

Continuing rumors that the Jewish Agency was on the verge of accepting a military armistice induced Sharett, the foreign minister-designate of the proposed Jewish state, to write Marshall in order to dispel this "persistent misunderstanding." "Indeed," Sharett explained, "I must emphasize that I had indicated all along that the provision for deferring the proclamation of a sovereign state was a major obstacle" to a truce arrangement. Sharett stressed that there could be "no prospect of an agreement which would preclude the setting up of a Provisional Government for the Jewish state. . . ." [10]

The Arabs stated that they would agree to a truce only on the basis of preservation of a unitary Arab state in Palestine and an immediate cessation of all Jewish immigration into the Holy Land. If any attempt were made to establish a sovereign Jewish state, the Arabs were pledged to destroy it, regardless of what the United Nations and the United States intended to do.[11]

On April 1, 1948, the Security Council voted to convene a special session of the General Assembly "to consider further the question of the future government of Palestine." Another Security Council resolution, also sponsored by the United States, called upon the warring parties in Palestine to agree to armistice terms. Representatives of the Jewish Agency and the Arab Higher Committee were asked to confer with the Security Council to arrange the truce.[12]

Implementation of an armistice in the Middle East was the first step in the American plan to set up a temporary trusteeship in Palestine. Once Arab and Jewish spokesmen met under United Nations auspices, however, it became obvious that the entire United States program was in serious difficulty.

There appeared to be no acceptable compromise regarding the establishment of a Jewish state. A truce seemed unattainable, and without it the trusteeship plan could not be carried out.[13]

Shortly after the special session opened on April 16, 1948, it was apparent that the United States proposal had failed to win much enthusiasm from various delegations. The Americans tried to persuade other member nations to agree to supply the necessary troops to keep order during the proposed trusteeship. In spite of an offer by the United States to share the responsibility, no other country was willing to offer troops.[14]

With the increasing unlikelihood of an armistice, critics of the United States trusteeship plan argued that it would take more military force to impose the new American plan than it would to carry out partition.[15]

American supporters of the trusteeship scheme were hopeful that Great Britain could be persuaded to assist in implementing the plan by agreeing to remain in Palestine beyond May 15, 1948. London, however, insisted its responsibility in the Holy Land would cease when the mandate ended. Since Palestine was already divided into Jewish and Arab areas corresponding approximately to the proposed boundaries in the partition plan, Britain recommended that the United Nations drop all efforts to impose any type of control and instead recognize accomplished facts.[16] In spite of the cool reception, State Department officials inexplicably believed as late as May 8, 1948, that it was still possible for a trusteeship plan to be passed by the General Assembly.[17] More realistic United Nations observers maintained that by early May the American plan was dead.[18]

Even had an armistice been accepted and sufficient troops lined up to serve during the trusteeship, there is no certainty that the American plan would have received United Nations approval. Member nations were at no time enthusiastic about the proposed trusteeship; only three or four delegations vigorously endorsed the plan. Many of the delegates wanted the Security Council to implement the original partition scheme.[19] One Latin American delegate attending the session later wrote that "a strange lethargy overtook the United Nations" in late April and early May. An increasingly dangerous civil conflict continued unabated in the Middle East, but nothing seemed to move the world organization.[20] A few days before the termination of Britain's mandate, time officially ran out for America's trusteeship proposal. No one in the General Assembly expressed regret when, on May 12, the United States dropped its support of the plan. The new American policy recommended simple recognition of the existence of Jewish and Arab areas in Palestine, and called upon the United Nations to act as mediator for a possible truce.[21]

By blocking Security Council attempts to implement partition, and subsequently proposing the alternative trusteeship plan, the United States was roundly criticized by advocates of a strong United Nations.[22] Critics noted that by responding to Arab threats with an offer to reexamine Palestine policy, the United States was damaging the credibility of the United Nations to enforce its decisions.[23] Years later, Secretary-General Lie wrote that the American "reversal was a blow to the United Nations and showed a profoundly disheartening disregard for its effectiveness and standing." Shaken by the United States shift, Lie began to doubt "what the future of the United Nations would be, if this was the measure of support it could expect from the United States."[24]

Much of the blame for the United Nations' inability to act in April and early May, 1948, must be assigned to the United States. In mid-April the Palestine Commission again issued an ominous call for Security Council assistance to stop a growing civil war in Palestine. All five members of the commission joined in predicting that "administrative chaos, starvation, widespread strife, violence, and bloodshed" would engulf the Holy Land unless the Security Council provided adequate military force before May 15.[25] When the United States blocked consideration, however, the Security Council could not fulfill the request.[26]

America's new Palestine policy proved to be a dismal failure. Proposed trusteeship was unable to gain even minimal support from member states. No other country offered to join the United States in supplying the troops needed to carry out the trusteeship. American diplomats maintained that trusteeship could be implemented only after an armistice, yet State Department assurances that a truce could be obtained proved incorrect. Faith in the ability of the United Nations to enforce its own decisions suffered, and the prestige of the United States within the world organization fell as a result. With full-scale war on the brink of eruption in the Middle East, America's shift in policy left the United Nations without the capacity to react.

CLARK CLIFFORD OUTLINES
THE CAMPAIGN STRATEGY

Clark McAdams Clifford, then thirty-eight years old, arrived in Washington in 1945 to serve in a relatively minor position as assistant to the president's naval aide. By June 1946 Truman was so pleased with the performance of the young St. Louis lawyer that he appointed him special counsel to the president. In his new post Clifford was responsible for, among other things, preparing many of Truman's state papers, public speeches, and private memoranda.[27]

Once at the fulcrum of power, according to Patrick Anderson in his study of presidential aides, Clifford displayed an "intelligence, subtlety, and instinct for power [that earned] him a place with [Harry] Hopkins, [Sherman] Adams, [Theodore] Sorenson, and [William] Moyers among the most influential of all White House aides." Clifford "swiftly became Harry Truman's most influential all-round adviser and, as such, one of the four or five most important White House aides in history."

Clifford, labeled the "Golden Boy" of the administration, and the homespun Truman seemed to be an unlikely personal and political team. An elegant, handsome, and charming man, Clifford appeared to have stepped onto the Washington "political stage [straight] from one of Scott Fitzgerald's stories." Yet from the outset Truman not only got along well with Clifford, but also developed an admiration and respect for his counsel. "The whole relationship between the President and me," Clifford later noted, "was a highly personal one. It developed because there was a vacuum in the White House. We were both from Missouri. He was comfortable with me." Anderson wrote that Clifford "must rank as one of the most successful —perhaps the most successful—of all the talented and ambitious men who have struggled in the shadows of presidential power." [28]

With the enthusiastic support of the president, Clifford prepared a memorandum outlining, in general terms, a proposed Democratic strategy for the 1948 presidential election. Clifford presented the forty-three-page document to the president in mid-November 1947. This bold political report, "The Politics of 1948," shows Clifford to be a tough political pragmatist. Tracing a proposed "course of political conduct" for the president to follow, Clifford informed Truman that the comments made in the memorandum "are based solely on an appraisal of the politically advantageous course to follow." [29] Truman carefully studied the document and in general agreed with Clifford's analysis and proposed strategy for victory. The memorandum became the blueprint for the 1948 campaign waged by Truman.[30]

Clifford correctly predicted that Governor Dewey would win the Republican nomination, and that Henry Wallace would run as a candidate for a third party. One serious miscalculation resulted from Clifford's inability to foresee the Dixiecrat movement. It was assumed in the memorandum that the president would have little difficulty carrying the South. In order to blunt support for Wallace, it was suggested that Truman move to the left on domestic issues. Clifford urged that the president keep Roosevelt's New Deal coalition together by appealing for votes among laborers, farmers, Negroes, and Catholics.[31]

One section of the memorandum dealt with the various special interest groups that the Democrats hoped to attract, including the Jewish community. Clifford's analysis of the Jewish vote is interesting because of its dual nature. On the one hand, Clifford outlined the political importance of securing Jewish voters during the 1948 campaign. In conclusion, however, he backed off from a recommendation that Palestine policy be determined on the basis of what would appeal to Jewish voters. Writing at a time when the United Nations was debating UNSCOP's partition proposal, Clifford believed that an attempt to use the Palestine issue to influence Jewish voters could possibly backfire. The pertinent section of Clifford's memorandum read:

> The Jewish vote . . . is important only in New York. But (except for Wilson in 1916) no candidate since 1876 has lost New York and won the Presidency, and its forty-seven [electoral] votes are naturally the first prize in any election. Centered in New York City, that vote is normally Democratic and, if large enough, is sufficient to counteract the upstate vote and deliver the state to President Truman. Today the Jewish bloc is interested primarily in Palestine and will continue to be an uncertain quantity right up to the time of election. Even though there is general approval among the Jewish people regarding the United Nations [Special Committee on Palestine's] report on Palestine, the group is still torn with conflicting views and dissension. It will be extremely difficult to decide some of the vexing questions which will arise in the months to come on the basis of political expediency. In the long run, there is likely to be greater gain if the Palestine problem is approached on the basis of reaching decisions founded upon intrinsic merit.[32]

When the memorandum was written, a full year before the election, Clifford was not convinced that the way to win the Jewish vote was by adopting policies in regard to Palestine solely on the basis of trying to please the Jews. As election day neared, however, Clifford apparently shifted his position. While continuing to believe that the Jewish vote could be a decisive factor in the election, he no longer accepted the idea that the Palestine policy of the administration could not be adapted to capture the Jewish vote. I hope to show in the following chapters that throughout 1948 Clifford recommended policies on the Palestine issue that were intended to improve the president's standing with the American Jewish community. Beginning in May, and extending to the election in November, the president's decisions on Palestine bore the mark of Clifford's influence. It appears that as the election drew nearer, Truman was increasingly willing to accept recommendations based upon domestic political considerations.

POLITICAL IMPLICATIONS OF REVERSAL

Truman's pro-Zionist advisers, Clifford and Niles in particular, were aware of the president's drift toward acceptance of the State Department argument that increasing tension between the Soviet Union and the United States necessitated postponing any showdown in Palestine. Since the proposed trusteeship plan was recommended to Truman as the one urgent Palestine alternative that would satisfy the national security, White House political counselors found it difficult to oppose.[33] In the immediate wake of the announcement of reversal, Clifford, Niles, Democratic national chairman Howard McGrath, and Federal Security Agency Administrator Oscar Ewing attempted to salvage some semblance of Jewish favor by proposing that the American arms embargo to the Middle East be lifted. These efforts, however, proved unsuccessful.[34]

Although angered by the unexpected timing of the announcement, Truman did not waver in his public endorsement
of the American reversal. On March 25, 1948, six days after
Austin's announcement, the White House released a presidential statement attempting to explain the shift. Written by Clifford, the presidential document said that the new American
plan was intended to stop violence and bloodshed from de-
scending upon the Holy Land. Large-scale fighting in Palestine
was viewed as imperiling the peace of the entire world. According to the statement, "trusteeship was proposed only after
we [the United States] had exhausted every effort to find a
way to carry out partition by peaceful means." [35] Since the Security Council was prevented from implementing partition by
American resistance, the presidential statement was not convincing.[36]

Public reaction to the American reversal was unfavorable.
A *New York Times* editorial argued that the administration's
new policy came "as a climax to a series of moves which has
seldom been matched, for ineptness, in the handling of any
international issue by an American Administration." [37] A
number of politicians in both parties assailed Truman's shift.
Governor Dewey curtly summed up the Democratic
administration's approach as "vacillating and inadequate."
Thirty Republican members of the House of Representatives
called for an immediate congressional investigation of the reversal.[38] Even within the president's own party, the criticism
was harsh. Congressman Celler insisted that "no more shame-
ful decision in international politics has ever been made by the
United States." [39] Another Democrat, New York Representative Arthur G. Klein, labeled the reversal "the most terrible
sellout of the common people since Munich." [40]

The overwhelming sentiment expressed in the correspondence directed at the president was extremely hostile to the
new Palestine policy. During the spring of 1948, the telegrams
received at the White House in response to the government's reversal opposed the new policy by a margin of twenty-two to

one.[41] A good deal of the correspondence resulted from Zionist-sponsored mail campaigns.[42]

POLITICAL PROBLEMS IN NEW YORK

Concerned with the unpleasant political implications of the reversal, Clifford got in touch with supporters of the Jewish cause in the weeks following Austin's announcement. Clifford was determined to keep the administration from losing the political support of these men, many of whom were influential liberals, and he encouraged them not to be discouraged with Truman. Apparently acting on his own, Clifford asked them to work to regain the president's support for a policy more consistent with Jewish goals in Palestine.[43]

The American reversal had clearly damaged Truman's standing within the Jewish community. Democrats were concerned about the consequences of this alienation in the November election. Jack Redding, publicity director for the Democratic National Committee, suggested at one strategy session that it was possible that Truman could be defeated for renomination by a revolt triggered in part by the unpopularity of the reversal.[44] The center of any revolt would have been New York, where Democratic leaders believed that displeased Jewish voters could bring about an electoral disaster. Leaders in the heavily Jewish districts began to comment that unless the situation changed, they could not support the president at the nominating convention. *New York Times* political writer Warren Moscow reported that several delegates from Jewish districts to the Democratic National Convention told their county chairmen that they did not feel they should have to vote for Truman at the convention. Moscow wrote that several party leaders in New York State were known to be hoping for a "northern revolt" that would persuade Truman not to make the race for reelection.[45] In mid-April 1948, the Democratic State Committee could not decide whether or not to endorse the president's bid for renomination.[46] Two state Democratic leaders bluntly warned Truman that "unless the calamitous and un-American policy is immediately reversed we shall do everything in our power to see to it that the Democratic Party rejects your candidacy at the forthcoming Democratic National Convention."[47]

Delegates attending an annual meeting of the Hebrew Sheltering and Immigrant Aid Society further indicated the extent of Jewish dissatisfaction with the president. Governor Dewey's message to the fifteen hundred assembled members was politely applauded, but the reading of a statement from Truman was "greeted with hisses and boos."[48]

Following the American reversal, the Zionists campaigned to induce Truman to shift his Palestine policy once again. One rally in New York City, summoned to protest the trusteeship plan, attracted over one hundred thousand sympathizers. Police authorities said it constituted the largest crowd ever to gather in Madison Square Garden. Ten days later, thirty thousand supporters attended a similar gathering at Yankee Stadium.[49]

Hoping to isolate himself from the pressure, the president refused to receive any spokesmen on the Palestine issue.[50] When Chaim Weizmann wrote to Truman with a plea not to abandon the cause of the Jews in Palestine, the Jewish leader's letter was not even answered.[51] Writing to pro-Zionist Congressman Sol Bloom, the president confided that the Palestine problem discouraged him. Truman said that finding an equitable solution "is almost an impossible job because of emotional factors which enter into the settlement. . . ."[52]

American Zionists had little reason to be encouraged in the weeks following the reversal. Late in April 1948, however, there was some evidence that Truman had not completely abandoned efforts to win their favor. The more optimistic Zionists predicted that the president was indicating that he was not satisfied with the results of the State Department policy he had accepted. This reappraisal was signaled by the appointment on April 28 of John Hilldring, a long-time supporter of a Jewish state, as a special assistant to Secretary of State Marshall for Palestine affairs.[53]

Future events would vindicate those who argued that Truman was to make yet another major reversal of America's Palestine policy.

9

American Recognition of Israel

FAILURE OF STATE
DEPARTMENT RECOMMENDATIONS

Early in May 1948 it became increasingly evident that the State Department's proposal for trusteeship was not going to pave the way for a pacification of the Holy Land. As the level of Jewish–Arab hostility continued to rise, the department's optimistic prognosis of a truce was not convincing.[1] Specific miscalculations by State Department officials further taxed their credibility. The pro-Zionist White House aides who were urging an alternative approach benefited each time the department's advice on the Palestine question was discredited.

One unfortunate misstep was taken when Secretary of State Marshall told an off-the-record press conference on April 28, 1948, that an armistice agreement had virtually been reached in the Middle East. One day later, Moshe Sharett, the foreign minister–designate of the Jewish state, wrote Marshall to "clear up [this] serious misunderstanding." Sharett pointed out that he had recently "expressed great scepticism" about the proposed truce arrangement to an American diplomat. His countrymen were opposed because the terms deferred establishment of a Jewish state.[2] On May 7, Sharett again wrote Marshall to put to rest the reports which he understood were "still current within the State Department and the White House to the effect that I [Sharett] had agreed to conditions for a military truce and political standstill in Palestine. . . ." Sharett emphasized that he "had indicated all along" that an armistice arrangement in its present form was unacceptable.[3]

A conversation between Clark Clifford and Dean Rusk on May 8, 1948, revealed a misunderstanding related to the status of America's proposed trusteeship plan. Rusk, director of the State Department's Office of Special Political Affairs, told Clifford that obtaining a truce was the department's foremost aim in Palestine. Even if it proved impossible to secure an armistice, Rusk confided, the votes were available in the General Assembly to pass a simplified version of the trusteeship proposal.[4] Rusk's source of information was certainly questionable, for by May 8 the trusteeship plan had been thoroughly discredited by United Nations members. Within a few days the United States abandoned its sponsorship of the scheme.[5]

Concerned with Truman's uphill campaign to win the presidency in 1948, Clifford believed the Jewish vote in New York State could be crucial.[6] Accordingly, he kept in close touch with supporters of the Zionist cause in an effort to encourage them to continue the crusade to persuade the president to adopt a more favorable policy toward the Jews in Palestine. Samuel I. Rosenman, a former Truman aide and an ally of the Zionists, was anxious for Clifford to inform the president that the State Department's proposed truce was not going to be accepted by the Jewish Agency. It was the hope of the Zionists that Truman would abandon the State Department's call for a truce and would instead endorse implementation of partition on May 15. Enclosing documents which detailed the agency's rejection of the truce, Rosenman noted that his enclosures "indicate very forceibly [*sic*] that [Moshe Sharett] did not agree to the truce as outlined by Mr. Rusk or the State Department. . . . I am sending you an original and a copy of these documents in the event that you find it desirable to give one to the President." [7] Another good friend of the Jewish Agency, Max Lowenthal, sent confidential memoranda to Clifford which urged a more positive American role in creating the Jewish state. For example, in one of the two messages written on May 7, Lowenthal wrote: *"FOR MR. CLIFFORD*

ONLY. This is, for the protection of the Administration, not to be shown in written form, to anyone else, *under any circumstances*." Arguing that Truman should not stand by a foreign policy that would prove politically harmful, Lowenthal suggested that the United States recognize the Jewish state even before May 15. Apparently referring to Republican criticism of American policy, Lowenthal believed that early recognition would "free the Administration of a serious and unfair disadvantage" in the 1948 election.[8]

Clifford was also able to use his sensitive White House position to encourage the president to accept a Palestine policy that gave the Zionists what they desired. By early May the Zionists had made clear what they wanted from the president of the United States. Truman was asked by the Zionists, and their supporters, to extend recognition promptly to the sovereign Jewish state once it came into existence.[9]

Chaim Weizmann's appeal to the president is representative of the manner in which the Zionists made their request. Hopeful of reversing the recently unfriendly posture of the White House, Weizmann began his letter by arguing that "the unhappy events of the last few months [should not] obscure the very great contributions" Truman had made to the cause of establishing a Jewish state. Recommending that the United States "promptly recognize the Provisional Government of the new Jewish state," Weizmann concluded by adding that he "would regard it as especially appropriate that the greatest living democracy should be the first to welcome the newest into the family of nations." [10]

Jewish spokesmen, as well as Democratic leaders, made certain that the president was aware of the enthusiasm for prompt recognition. While conferring with the president on May 12, 1948, Congressman Sol Bloom, the ranking Democrat on the House Committee on Foreign Affairs, suggested to Truman that he should arrange to have the United States become the first nation to recognize the Jewish state.[11] When

Democratic leader Joseph F. Guffey forwarded a letter to Truman from a delegate to the Democratic National Convention who sought prompt American recognition of the Jewish state, Truman replied: "You'd be surprised how many letters of this sort I get and how easy it is for people on the outside to settle this almost insoluble question." [12]

Advice on the political implications of the Palestine situation was freely given to the president by Democrats. The specific political counsel offered to Truman by Chicago's leading Democratic figure, Jacob M. Arvey, provides an example of the messages received at the White House. Arvey wrote Truman to discuss the "political repercussions implicit" in the establishment of a Jewish state. "I fear very much," he confided, "that the Republicans are planning to exploit the present situation to their further advantage. This ought not to be permitted." A nationwide series of Jewish rallies had been planned for May 16, 1948, to hail what would then be the day-old State of Israel. "Only a declaration [of American recognition of the new state] by [Truman] before Sunday evening [the scheduled time of the rallies]," Arvey contended, "can transform the sentiments of the multitudes who are certain to attend these meetings from bitter criticism to unparalleled laudation." If a friendly act toward the new state were delayed until after public enthusiasm had been exhibited by the mass meetings, "the Republicans will claim that the public opinion which they helped to arouse forced your hand." A statement of American recognition, "timely made, will turn millions to hail you as the champion of justice for the most sorely tried people on the face of the earth." [13]

There was some evidence that the Republicans were hoping to use the Palestine situation to their political advantage. Senator Robert Taft, a Republican with serious presidential ambitions, announced that if he were in a position to act, he would recognize the Jewish state when it proclaimed its independence on May 15, 1948.[14]

Using their positions within the White House, both Clifford and Niles offered Truman political advice that was boldly aimed at recapturing the favor of the Jewish community. On the morning of May 6, 1948, the two aides conferred. They were inclined toward the possibility of a presidential statement to be issued before May 15, announcing the government's intention to recognize the Jewish state formally as soon as it came into being. Shortly after the meeting with Clifford, Niles prepared a draft of a proposed presidential statement along the lines they had discussed. Niles included the text of the draft in the following memorandum he sent to Clifford:

Here is a first draft of the proposed statement along the lines you and I talked about this morning. I had Ben Cohen [an adviser to the State Department] over here and asked him to read it, and it has his complete approval. I will try to get the reaction of a few other people. [The draft reads:] "During this period events in Palestine have outstripped our efforts for a peaceful solution. There has been much bloodshed and disorder. Nevertheless, despite this bloodshed and disorder, a significant development has occurred. The partition solution which could not be enforced by external means has now become a practical reality in Palestine. After a most exhaustive review of all angles of the situation, Secretary Marshall and I [Truman] have concluded that we should recognize this practical reality, since it conforms to the resolution of the United Nations, to the security interests of the United States, and to the announced and oft repeated objective of the United States Government. We intend, therefore, to accord formal recognition to the Jewish Government in Palestine when it is established, as I understand it will be on May 16th [sic]. We hope that we may be able to take a similar action with regard to an Arab Government in the Arab area of Palestine." [15]

Clifford presented this possible approach to Truman six days later, during a crucial conference on the Palestine issue.

THE WHITE HOUSE
CONFRONTATION ON RECOGNITION

By May 12, 1948, all hope had vanished that an armistice could stop a full-scale war from exploding in Palestine once the mandate ended. It was also apparent that the United Nations was not going to approve a provisional regime, such as trusteeship, before May 15, Accordingly, the United Nations resolution of November 29, 1947, was still in force. Spokesmen for the Jewish Agency announced that on May 15, 1948, the Jews would proclaim a sovereign Jewish state in accordance with the boundaries established in the partition resolution. Arab League officials stated that they would set up a single Arab civil administration throughout Palestine on the same day. A Jewish–Arab war loomed as the manner in which the question of the control of Palestine would be resolved.[16]

A White House conference on Palestine was convened on May 12, 1948, to discuss what action the United States should take once the British mandate terminated. Along with the president, the six others in attendance were White House aides Clifford and Niles, and Marshall, Robert Lovett, Robert McClintock, and Fraser Wilkins, a veteran foreign service officer, all representing the State Department. For almost an hour and a half the president listened attentively to the alternative proposals. It appeared to those present that Truman had not yet determined which direction to take.[17]

Clifford argued that the president should announce the American intention of recognizing the Jewish state even before it came into existence. Adoption of this policy, Clifford said, would be consistent with the president's past endorsement of the establishment of a Jewish state in Palestine. Clifford emphasized that his support for such a policy was firmly based upon a consideration of the favorable political implications involved. With an election six months away, Truman should not pass up the opportunity to redeem his fallen reputation in the Jewish community. Niles, who was satisfied to let Clifford make the case for a policy they both favored, spoke very little during the conference. One participant, Robert McClintock, later noted that "Clifford argued entirely on grounds of domestic politics." [18]

Undersecretary of State Robert Lovett contributed much of the opposition to Clifford's argument. According to Lovett, in international law it would be wrong to recognize prematurely the existence of a new state, for any such recognition would be considered interference in the functioning of an already existing state. Lovett recommended that the United States adopt a "wait and see" policy toward the Jewish state. Once the new government demonstrated its administrative control of the territory, thus meeting the same test that would be applied to any new government, the United States would consider formal recognition. To allow an exception in this case, Lovett warned, would antagonize future American–Arab relations. He cautioned against sacrificing the nation's long-range foreign policy goals for a momentary political gain. [19]

Clifford and Lovett, each representing a distinctly different approach, did most of the talking at the conference. It was a serious, sober discussion, not one marked by emotional outbursts. Marshall, who had remained relatively uninvolved with the Palestine issue while serving as secretary of state, said almost nothing at the session. [20] Loy Henderson and Carlton Savage, both State Department officials in 1948, have confirmed in interviews with the author that Lovett often acted in Marshall's name on the Palestine issue. Marshall did not wish to become involved in the Palestine question because he disliked the frequent intrusion of domestic politics into decisions that were made. [21] At one point in the conference, however, Marshall challenged Clifford's recommendations. The secretary of state strongly appealed to Truman not to decide Palestine policy on the basis of domestic politics. Clifford's very presence at the conference, Marshall said, indicated an intention to involve local politics in what was a serious question of foreign policy.[22] As the session ended, Truman had still not indicated what policy he was inclined to follow.[23]

After the White House conference, Lovett arranged to have Clifford receive a memorandum from the State Department's legal adviser, Ernest A. Gross. Any premature recognition of a new state's existence, the memorandum noted, "is wrongful in international law because such recognition constitutes an unwarranted interference in the affairs of the previously existing state." Gross also outlined the department's criteria for extending recognition. Even waiting until the day that the Jewish state came into being, and then immediately thereafter extending recognition, would not meet the department's standard requirements.[24]

THE DECISION
FOR IMMEDIATE RECOGNITION

Truman apparently made up his mind sometime between the conclusion of the conference on May 12 and the morning of May 14. He decided to adopt a politically beneficial Palestine policy, presumably on the advice offered by political adviser Clifford. Instead of making any announcement before the mandate ended, however, Truman insisted upon issuing formal recognition only moments after the Jewish state came into existence. Before noon on Friday, May 14, he summoned Clifford and told him to make the necessary arrangements for recognition later that afternoon. Clifford telephoned Eliahu Epstein, the Jewish Agency's representative in Washington, and informed him of Truman's intention. Before American recognition could be extended, however, a request for it was required from the new state. Clifford wanted to know the precise time when the proclamation of independence would become effective, and if it would be a "provisional government" that would be formed.[25] When he learned that the government would be "provisional in nature," plans were made to make the recognition de facto rather than de jure.[26] In an effort to guard against having the story prematurely leaked to the press, Clifford demanded and received a "pledge of secrecy" from Epstein. Since this pledge precluded "wide consultation and prior notification" of Jewish officials in Palestine, Epstein assumed full responsibility for making the formal request for recognition.[27] During the afternoon of May 14, Epstein delivered the following message to the White House and to the State Department:

> I have the honor to notify you that the state of Israel has been proclaimed as an independent republic. . . . The Act of Independence will become effective one minute after six o'clock in the evening of 14 May 1948, Washington time. . . . I have been authorized by the provisional government of the new state to tender this message and to express the hope that your government will recognize and will welcome Israel into the community of nations.[28]

Meanwhile, at the White House, Clifford was finishing the preparations for American recognition. He telephoned Loy Henderson, director of the State Department's Office of Near Eastern and African Affairs, to verify that the boundaries of the new state were in accordance with the boundaries approved in the United Nations partition resolution.[29] Lovett, who was responsible for drafting the American statement of recognition, delegated the task to Robert McClintock.[30]

Later in the afternoon of May 14, Epstein attempted to get in touch with Clifford in order to assure himself that the situation was under control. The telephone lines were tied up for some time, but Epstein was finally able to get through at about 5:30 P.M. A White House aide told Epstein to relax—all the preparations had been taken care of.[31]

Britain's mandate expired at precisely 6:00 P.M., Washington time (which was midnight in Palestine). To symbolize Great Britain's withdrawal, the Union Jack was hauled down and

British High Commissioner Sir Alan Cunningham sailed off from the port of Haifa. In a solemn ceremony at the Tel Aviv Museum of Art, the sovereign Jewish state of Israel was proclaimed.[32]

At 6:11 P.M., Truman's press secretary, Charles G. "Charlie" Ross, released the following White House statement:

> This Government has been informed that a Jewish state has been proclaimed in Palestine and recognition has been requested by the provisional government thereof. The United States recognizes the provisional government as the de facto authority of the new State of Israel.[33]

REACTION TO AMERICAN RECOGNITION

Within the announcement of Israel's independence, spontaneous explosions of joy were recorded in New York's Jewish sections. Groups of men linked arms in the street and danced the hora, an Israeli folk dance. Strains of "Hatikvah," the Zionist anthem, were heard throughout the city. When the news of United States recognition reached the blacked-out city of Tel Aviv, the effect "was electric." Late celebrants in the coffeehouses poured into the streets, "shouting, cheering and toasting the United States." [34]

A less enthusiastic response occurred at the General Assembly headquarters at Lake Success. Wire service reports of the White House statement reached the United Nations at about 6:30 P.M., and were immediately passed around from delegate to delegate. The *New York Times* reported that at first the "reaction was that someone was making a terrible joke, and some diplomats broke into skeptical laughs." [35] One delegate mounted the rostrum and asked if the American delegation could give the assembly a verification of the report. Francis B. Sayre, the United States representative on the Trusteeship Council, replied that for the time being he had no official information.[36]

No hint had been given to the American mission of White House plans to extend immediate recognition to Israel. Taken by surprise, the bewildered American delegates telephoned the State Department for confirmation.[37] One half hour later, American delegate Philip C. Jessup read the text of the statement of recognition to the General Assembly.[38] United Nations officials, delegates, and the sparse group of visitors "were dumbfounded . . . and few believed it at first." Many delegates showed "considerable resentment" over the manner in which the United States had pressed hard for the trusteeship plan, only to reverse herself and implicitly approve the partition scheme by recognizing Israel. George Barrett of the *New York Times* reported that when one delegate was asked for the United States position on Palestine, he replied that he did not know because he had not seen an announcement for twenty minutes. Barrett, who did not identify the delegate, noted that "most remarks heard around the corridors were too caustic to be attributed to the authors." When asked for his reaction, New Zealand representative Carl Berendsen replied, "Just dizzy, that's all, just dizzy." [39]

Failure by the United Nations either to repeal partition or provide adequate military force to keep the peace meant that the fate of Palestine was left to the outcome of the Jewish–Arab war. The extent of the General Assembly's efforts toward a peaceful solution was a last-moment decision to send a United Nations mediator to Palestine to try to arrange a truce and carry on public services. Having accomplished little during the special session, the General Assembly adjourned on the evening of May 14.[40]

Minutes after the White House statement on recognition had been released, Truman telephoned Niles and said: "Dave, I want you to know that I've just announced recognition. You're the first person I've called, because I knew how much this would mean to you." [41] It would appear the the president wanted to inform Niles immediately of the recognition of Israel because he knew that his administrative assistant would be delighted to hear the news after waging so long a struggle for just such an action. Yet among Truman's aides, Niles had not been the most influential one in convincing the president that he should recognize Israel just minutes after it came into being. In the fall of 1946, Niles had led the campaign to line up presidential endorsement for a Jewish state. By 1948, however, Clifford overshadowed whatever influence on Palestine policy Niles enjoyed. Whereas Niles was used in the limited role of the administration's informal representative to the Jewish community, Clifford had a broader and far more important position as the president's special counsel. It was Clifford who made the successful presentation for immediate recognition of Israel at the conference of May 12, 1948, and he was also the adviser to whom Truman turned on May 14 in order to carry out the plans for immediate recognition. Functioning as the president's chief political counselor, Clifford emerged in the election year of 1948 as the person most responsible for American policy in the Middle East.

Public reaction to Truman's decision to recognize Israel was mostly favorable. A survey of newspaper editorial opinion made by the writer indicated general approval of the president's motives for issuing formal recognition just eleven minutes after the British mandate expired. Of the eighty-five large-circulation newspapers surveyed, forty-one published editorials that assigned a motive to Truman's prompt recognition: twenty-four (59 percent) considered that he was taking a logical and proper step by merely acknowledging that the state of Israel did exist; fourteen (34 percent) indicated he was trying to encourage Jewish political support; twelve (29 percent) attributed his action to a desire to beat the Soviet Union and become the first nation to recognize the Jewish state; [42] three (7 percent) inferred that humanitarian reasons ruled his decision (Jews had suffered enough); and one (2 percent) felt that Truman wanted to demonstrate America's faith in freedom. [43]

Jewish leaders were unanimous in their praise of the president. Sharett, who had been highly critical of the administration, now thanked Truman for his "momentous and significant" act. David Ben-Gurion, who became Israel's first prime minister, applauded the president for his "great gesture." [44] Other friends of the Israeli cause, as well as the Democratic leadership, took the opportunity to express their approval.[45] One observer noted that when American recognition was made public, it was "difficult to describe the prayers and praise in the synagogue that were showered on President Truman . . . , who, once again, has been taken to the heart and bosom of Israel." [46] References to the president were cheered by a capacity crowd of nineteen thousand at a "Salute to Israel" rally at Madison Square Garden in New York City on May 16.[47]

In March 1948, Truman had indicated a willingness to accept the political repercussions of a Palestine policy that was unfavorable to the Jews provided he was convinced the national security necessitated such a policy. Subsequently, however, he had learned that following State Department advice could be politically risky, and what is more the proposed trusteeship plan had failed to provide a solution to Palestine's problems. By the time he was called on to make another Palestine decision, his confidence in the State Department had apparently been shaken by its prior miscalculations. On the other hand, whether Truman decided to recognize Israel on May 14 or several weeks later did not appear to involve the national security or imperil world peace. By following Clifford's advice, the president could give a boost to his political fortunes. Conformity to the traditional State Department procedure of recognition was not as important to Truman in May 1948 as obtaining a solid political base within the Jewish community.

10

A Pro-Zionist Mood in Washington

THE ATTEMPTS TO HALT
THE ARAB-ISRAELI WAR

Only hours after the Israeli proclamation of independence, a full-scale war was raging in the Middle East as Arab forces launched a massive assault to "liberate the Holy Land from Zionism." By noon on May 15, 1948, enemy planes were swooping down on targets in the Israeli capital of Tel Aviv.[1] At the United Nations, Secretary-General Lie was concerned that unless the conflict could be halted immediately, the war would spread to other countries. Writing to each permanent Security Council member, Lie pointed out that for the first time since the adoption of the United Nations Charter, member states "have openly declared that they have engaged in armed intervention outside their own territory." A clear need existed, the secretary-general stated, for the Security Council to "take a decisive stand in support of the authority of the Charter and of the United Nations."[2]

On May 22 the Security Council adopted a resolution that demanded a comprehensive cease-fire within thirty-six hours. Although Israeli acceptance was received, the Arab states initially rejected participation in the proposed truce.[3] The Arabs eventually agreed to the resolution following the strong diplomatic and political pressures adopted by those nations favoring an immediate cease-fire in the Middle East. After a delay resulting from differences between Israel and the Arab states over the interpretations of the Security Council's provisions, both sides finally agreed to accept a four-week armistice to begin June 11.[4]

Count Folk Bernadotte, the president of the Swedish Red Cross, who had been appointed the United Nations mediator by Lie, tried to secure an extension of the truce, but his efforts were rebuffed.[5] Following the firm Arab rejection of a continuation, the mediator reported on July 8 from his headquarters on the island of Rhodes that the "war is on again." [6] American representative Philip C. Jessup announced to the Security Council that unless the Arabs accepted cease-fire terms, the United States would support economic and diplomatic sanctions by the United Nations against the Arabs. According to Lie, it was the American threat of sanctions that induced the Arabs to yield. A second armistice accord, scheduled for an unlimited duration, went into effect on July 18.[7]

TRUMAN'S APPEAL
TO THE JEWISH COMMUNITY

Immediate United States recognition of Israel marked a turning point in Truman's approach to the Palestine-Israel issue. Until the president's unprecedented action on May 14, 1948, his policy had been one of vacillation. Beginning with diplomatic recognition of the Jewish state, Truman made a series of decisions favoring Israel. With the November election drawing near, the White House sought increasingly friendly relations with the American Jewish community through its policy toward Israel.

Chaim Weizmann's first official act as Israeli president was to accept Truman's invitation to be his guest in Washington. Arriving at the capital, the venerable statesman discovered that Pennsylvania Avenue was bedecked with the flags of the United States and Israel. During a White House conference on May 25, Weizmann was pleased to learn of the president's sympathetic concern with the problems that beset the embattled

Jewish state. When the possibility of a loan to Israel was discussed, Truman confidently told Weizmann that "there was no trouble about that because the Jews paid their debts." [8]

A month later the president further pleased the domestic supporters of Israel. On June 22 Truman convened a small group of his advisers to select the person to head the United States diplomatic mission in Tel Aviv. It was recommended by the State Department that the post be filled by a career foreign service officer. Truman, however, rejected the department's candidates for the position, and instead chose James G. McDonald, one of the members of the Anglo-American Committee of Inquiry who had clearly sympathized with the Zionist position while serving on that body. McDonald's work in assisting the Jewish refugees who had immigrated to Israel also commended him to the leadership of the new State. Clifford, who was asked to carry out the president's decision, telephoned McDonald to secure his acceptance.

At 4:20 P.M. that same day, Clifford telephoned Robert Lovett, the acting secretary of state, and reported that the president wanted the State Department to announce McDonald's appointment that evening. Lovett argued that this was impossible because an envoy could not be approved until he had been declared persona grata by the country to which he had been assigned. Clifford suggested that Lovett get in touch with Eliahu Epstein, the Israeli representative in Washington, and ask for the appropriate confirmation. Confiding to Lovett that McDonald's selection "delighted" him, Epstein immediately arranged for a formal notice of approval to be delivered to the State Department. An official announcement of McDonald's appointment as the Special Representative of the United States to Israel was issued less than three hours after Clifford asked McDonald to accept the position.[9] The speed and manner of handling McDonald's appointment clearly show that the entire matter was arranged by Clifford in the White House, and not through the standard procedures followed in the State Department.

The State Department made little effort to conceal its displeasure over McDonald's selection. During Clifford's telephone conversation with Lovett on the afternoon of the appointment, the acting secretary expressed his dissatisfaction with the decision "on the grounds of McDonald's identification with the Zionists and for other reasons." In reply, Clifford firmly said that "he did not want any discussion of the matter"; he only wanted the State Department to proceed with the preparations of the formal announcement.[10] Marshall, who had been hospitalized on May 22, later told McDonald that he was opposed to his nomination "because he strongly disliked having such an appointment announced before he could be given an opportunity for consultation or comment." [11] Reaction to McDonald's selection in Israel, and among American Jews, was far more friendly. Weizmann, for example, cabled his "heartfelt thanks" to Truman for a selection that brought "deep satisfaction to the community of Israel and to Jewry generally." [12] McDonald's appointment demonstrated that the White House, not the State Department, was deciding the administration's policy toward Israel. The procedures used in making the appointment also emphasized that Clifford was playing a major role in determining Israel policy.

In mid-July the Democratic National Convention adopted a platform plank that was in accord with the increasingly evident White House goal of solidifying the administration's political support within the Jewish community. Assigning to Truman a significant share of the credit for establishing the Jewish state, the platform pledged that the Democratic administration would extend a program of support and assistance to Israel. The Democrats, according to the platform, "affirm pride that the United States, under the leadership of President Truman, played a leading role" in the United Nations adoption of the partition resolution. They also applauded Truman's recognition of Israel. Past accomplishments, the platform pledged, would be joined with future contributions. A

Democratic administration would not agree to modification of Israel's boundaries, as had been suggested by some as a means of bringing peace to the Middle East, unless such changes were "fully acceptable" to the Jewish state. A promise to sponsor Israel's bid for United Nations membership was also made. The platform said that American financial aid should be offered to Israel to assist in the new nation's economic development. The arms embargo, according to the platform, should be lifted so that Israel could defend herself against aggression.[13]

Truman's relations with the American Jewish community had improved so greatly since the spring of 1948 that by the time the convention met, the threat of a revolt over the Palestine issue had vanished. New York State, where discussion of the political rebellion had centered, wound up casting all its ninety-eight votes for Truman in the balloting for a Democratic presidential nominee.[14]

CLIFFORD AND THE QUEST FOR JEWISH VOTES

Republican Thomas E. Dewey and Democrat Harry S. Truman emerged as the two major-party candidates for the presidency. Following the adjournment of the political conventions, the presidential campaign entered an intensified phase. Clifford was soon engaged in the uphill struggle to win reelection for the president. As he had done in the past, most notably in his memorandum on the 1948 election and in his presentation at the White House conference preceding recognition, Clifford continued to stress the value of the Jewish vote. Although the great majority of Jews had traditionally voted Democratic, President Truman could not fully count on their support. Leo Isacson's upset victory in the special Bronx congressional election of February 1948 had shown that Jews would switch to the candidate of another party if they were

displeased with the Palestine-Israel policies of the administration. American Labor party candidate Isacson's "militantly
pro-Palestine appeal" had combined with dissatisfaction over
Truman's failure to work enthusiastically for implementation
of partition to hold the Democrat Karl Propper to 31 percent
of the vote in the usually safe Democratic district—and Propper had strongly endorsed the Zionist program for Palestine.
Propper, then, was the victim of a negative Jewish reaction to
the Democratic administration's policy.[15]

Truman's swift recognition of Israel, however, and the
ensuing presidential acts of good will had combined to rally a
large segment of the Jewish community behind Truman. With
the election approaching, Clifford wanted to secure an even
larger share of Jewish support. By moving in a pro-Israeli
direction, there was little chance of alienating any substantial
bloc of voters in the United States, while such action could influence the size of the president's expected plurality among
Jewish voters. Among other factors, New York could be won
or lost depending on the size of the Jewish plurality; and with
forty-seven electoral votes, New York could decide which
candidate would become president.[16]

Eager to see Jewish requests translated into American policy, Clifford remained sensitive to the demands of Israel's
friends within the United States. He soon learned that most of
the attention was focused on three specific issues that could be
resolved in Israel's favor by positive presidential action. One
such appeal was for Truman to extend de jure, or full, recognition to Israel.[17] Greater urgency was attached to the request
for a hundred-million-dollar American loan to the Jewish
state. Weizmann stressed the importance of the loan during his
state visit to Washington in late May 1948. Truman's public
endorsement of the loan came shortly before the election. Privately, however, Truman gave assurance during the summer
that the loan would be made. Edward Jacobson spent a "very
lengthy visit" with the president on August 5, 1948, at which
time he asked Truman about the possibility of the United

States granting a loan to Israel. Writing to Weizmann, Jacobson said that Truman had "authorized me to tell you that he would give us action in the very near future." Jacobson suggested that it would be "wise" for Weizmann to "drop the President a note thanking him in advance for his assistance." [18] Weizmann followed Jacobson's advice; he wrote to the American president and offered his appreciation for the promise to grant a loan:

> I have just received from our friend, Mr. Eddie Jacobson, an account of the conversation which he was privileged to have with you a few weeks ago on the subject of the proposed loan to Israel. In his letter, Mr. Jacobson tells me that when he left you he felt confident of good news at an early date. May I now express my deep appreciation of the keen interest you have taken in the project? In sanctioning this loan, you will be giving assistance to those schemes of refugee welfare and economic and social development which have always attracted your interest in connection with Palestine and the Near East." [19]

Truman was also asked to lift the American arms embargo for the Middle East, allowing Israel to purchase weapons. "The finger of God points to You as a restorer of Israel," one pro-Zionist advocate wrote to Truman. "You must not falter [;] therefore follow up your act of recognition of Israel by lifting the embargo so that Israel may defend its life against the invading Arab carrying British weapons of destruction." [20] Unlike the first two issues, Jewish appeals to end the embargo were to remain unanswered. On December 5, 1947, the American arms embargo had been imposed at the request of the United Nations Security Council. Truman was persuaded by the State Department to believe that any unilateral revocation of the embargo would be regarded as exhibiting a striking disregard for United Nations efforts to pacify the Middle East.[21] Another compelling reason for presidential inaction derived from the public response to the embargo. Although the Zionist program generally met with either mild public approval or indifference, one nationwide poll indicated that 82 percent of the electorate opposed any change in the status of the embargo.[22]

By keeping in touch with the supporters of Israel, Clifford became a rallying point within the administration for those who sought further presidential action in behalf of the Jewish state.[23] Clifford gave assurances that the friends of Israel within the administration were waging a strenuous campaign to have the appropriate policies adopted. For example, in a letter to M. J. Slonim, an official of the American Jewish Congress, Clifford made clear his interest in Israel. He wrote that "those of us who are interested in aiding in every way the new state of Israel" were delighted over McDonald's selection to head the American mission. Regarding the possibility of securing de jure recognition for Israel, Clifford confided that there were members of the administration who were working on the problem: "Rest assured that we have this matter in mind and shall continue to work toward full recognition." [24] Clifford's rapport with the Jewish leadership is one indication that, apart from his interest in the political implications of White House support for the Zionist goals, he personally believed the cause was a just one. It is apparent, however, that during his contacts with the president on the issue, Clifford consistently stressed the political consequences of advocating a pro-Zionist stance.

During the campaign, the White House received information from Democrats relating to the potential political impact of a bold pro-Israeli policy upon the election. A letter to Clifford on September 23, 1948, from Chester Bowles, the party's candidate for governor in Connecticut, indicated the Democratic politician's apprehension concerning Jewish votes. "Like you and every one else who is concerned about November 2nd [election day]," Bowles wrote, "I am worried about the Jewish situation." He noted that "we have an ardent group of Zionists here in the State" who wanted Truman to extend de jure recognition to Israel. Bowles recommended that the president seize the initiative by issuing a sweeping statement that would not only grant full recognition, but would also offer American economic aid and a promise to sponsor Israel's bid for United Nations membership. He suggested that Truman state this new policy on September 30, the Jewish New Year, which "gives him an excellent excuse to make a statement of this kind. . . ." By postponing this message "until later in October, we will get no [Jewish] help as far as registration is concerned and the opposition will charge [Truman] with playing politics with our foreign policy." Bowles argued that some presidential move was required. "I really believe some action along this line is vital. I know how important it is in Connecticut; and if we are up against it here, it must be infinitely tougher in New York." [25]

According to New York Democrats, success in the election depended in large part on the extent of Truman's commitment to Israel. Two local party officials insisted that by adopting policies favorable to Israel, Truman "will swing New York State into the Democratic column. . . ." [26] A state senator from New York warned that the president would be "very vulnerable" in the state unless he made more of an effort to champion the cause of Israel." [27] Citizens who wrote to Truman advised him to assist Israel if he wanted to be reelected. One writer offered a dramatic formula: send planes and atomic bombs to the Israeli government.[28] Another correspondent predicted that by favoring the Jewish state, "you will get the vote of almost every Jew in America." [29] Clifford was clearly aware of the political need for a significant American commitment to Israel. In the weeks immediately preceding the election, he was determined to guide the president toward an Israeli policy that would win approval within the Jewish community.

11

Truman's Pre-election Appeal to American Jewry

MARSHALL PREMATURELY ENDORSES THE BERNADOTTE PLAN

While driving through the Israeli-held section of Jerusalem on September 17, 1948, the United Nations mediator, Count Bernadotte, was cut down by assassins' bullets.[1] Foreign Minister Moshe Sharett disclaimed any official Israeli responsibility for this brutal act of Jewish terrorists.[2] At the time of his death, Bernadotte had nearly completed a report containing his recommendations for a program to end the Arab-Jewish war. Three days after the assassination, the mediator's proposals for a compromise settlement were announced.

Bernadotte's plan included a major readjustment of Israel's boundaries in an effort to reduce friction points, a formal recognition of the Jewish state, and the guaranteed return of Arab refugees to the homes in Palestine they had fled. A particularly controversial aspect of the proposed settlement was the stipulation that the Negev, a desert area in southern Palestine, be removed from the Jewish state and given to the Arabs.[3]

Robert McClintock, the special assistant to Dean Rusk, head of the State Department's Office of Special Political Affairs, had consulted Bernadotte a short time before the assassination. McClintock cabled the State Department from Cairo to suggest that the emotional impact of Bernadotte's tragic end might possibly pave the way for the acceptance of his plan to end the war. During an ensuing session with Rusk,

McClintock proposed that the United States endorse the Bernadotte program as a way to bring peace to the Middle East. Rusk, who was receptive to the idea, sent it on to Marshall, who agreed that the assassination might be an opportunity for peace. Although the secretary of state had rarely been drawn into the Palestine issue, on this occasion he resolved to announce American endorsement of the Bernadotte report.[4]

Without seeking White House approval, Marshall issued a statement on September 21 that the United States "considers that the conclusions contained in the final report of Count Bernadotte offer a generally fair basis for settlement of the Palestine question." The Washington government, Marshall said, "is of the opinion that the conclusions are sound, and strongly urges the parties and the General Assembly to accept them in their entirety as the best possible basis for bringing peace to a distracted land." [5] Marshall's statement was contrary to the Democratic platform, which had endorsed the Israeli boundaries designated in the partition resolution. No border changes should be made, the platform stated, unless they were "fully acceptable" to the Jewish state.[6]

The government of Israel, in a firm rejection of Bernadotte's report, specifically criticized the proposed boundary revisions.[7] The Jews viewed the loss of the largely uninhabited Negev, which they hoped to settle and develop in the future, as intolerable. Withdrawal of the Negev would take away 3,200 square miles, and leave Israel with only 2,500 square miles for an estimated population of two million. In addition to its potential for resettlement and development, the Negev held considerable strategic importance for a small nation with no other buffer protecting it from its most powerful neighbor, Egypt. In a cable to Edward Jacobson, President Weizmann asked him to "please go and see [Truman] without delay, reminding him of Democratic Party pledge that no change in boundaries would take place without consent Government of Israel, but above all his own encouragement to me on which we all very implicit [l]y rely. . . ." [8]

TRUMAN DECIDES
AGAINST REPUDIATING MARSHALL

While aboard the president's campaign train, Truman and Clifford first learned of Marshall's acceptance of the Bernadotte plan.[9] News of the secretary of state's action discouraged Clifford and the president's other political aides. With one stroke, Marshall threatened to undo the political gains that had been so carefully acquired and nurtured within the Jewish community. Wary Jewish observers wanted to know if the government had once again reversed itself. The presidential party was inundated with criticism of the apparent abandonment of the Democratic platform's Israel plank.[10] Bartley Crum, who was concerned with these political implications, warned Clifford that "Marshall is doing [the] President more harm than anything I can think of." [11]

Hopeful of minimizing the political damage, Clifford got in touch with Undersecretary of State Lovett to explore the possibility of a modification of Marshall's endorsement. In a top-secret dispatch, Lovett reported that he had "discussed the matter with [the] Secretary in the light of your [Clifford's] comments and he is most anxious to be as helpful as possible." Marshall had expressed his willingness to use "alternative language" in reference to the Bernadotte plan.[12] After preparing a proposed presidential statement that would clearly have modified American enthusiasm for Bernadotte's report, Clifford sought and received Lovett's approval of the specific phrasing.[13] Before Clifford could convert his advance work into presidential policy, however, Truman had to be persuaded to make a public comment on Marshall's acceptance of the Bernadotte plan.

On September 28, 1948, when the Democratic campaign train pulled into Oklahoma City, the president held a lengthy meeting with his staff to decide what course of action should be adopted in order to keep any political losses to a minimum. Truman agreed to issue a statement reaffirming the Israel plank of the Democratic platform. He also issued instructions to have appropriate remarks prepared.[14] On the following day, Clifford finished the draft of a proposed presidential memorandum to Marshall that would inform him of Truman's planned statement. According to the draft, Marshall was told that "your statement that the Bernadotte report should be used as a basis for negotiation . . . requires clarification." Clifford's draft pointed out that the United States had supported the partition resolution "as to boundaries," and that the Democratic platform had also endorsed the existing Israeli borders. Of greatest significance was the memorandum's conclusion: "I shall have to state that my position as to boundaries has not changed. You should know that my statement will be made on October first." [15]

However, Truman changed his mind about issuing any statement on the Bernadotte plan at that time. In his *Memoirs,* Truman recalled that his decision not to comment was based on a desire not to publicly embarrass his secretary of state.[16] Probably a more significant reason was the president's belief that such a statement could lose votes. A general expectation was that both Dewey and Truman were to keep American foreign policy bipartisan, and therefore out of the campaign.[17] If the public were led to believe that a candidate violated this informal understanding on bipartisanship, it might have a negative political impact. A Truman political aide, William Boyle, Jr., explained in a memorandum why some of the president's advisers believed that the risks were too great to issue any remarks on the Bernadotte plan: "His [Truman's] enemies would attack anything he says and even his friends (or those who would agree with the statement) would discount it as political, coming at this time. . . . A Truman statement would lose more votes than it would get." [18] Although choosing not to comment on Marshall's acceptance of the Bernadotte report, Truman was determined to prevent any similar incident from embarrassing him. Accordingly, when the British and Chinese jointly proposed a fiercely anti-Israeli resolution in the United Nations, the president acted to insure that no member of the United States delegation would offer any American support. Truman issued the following order to the American mission: "I request that no statement be made or no action be taken on the subject of Palestine by any member of our delegation in Paris without obtaining specific authority from me and clearing the text of any statement." [19]

By mid-October the Democratic political prognosis in the wake of Marshall's action was not favorable. It was apparent that many Jews regarded Marshall's endorsement as yet another American reversal. Clifford learned that, as a result of that endorsement, Democratic Congressmen Emanuel Celler and Sol Bloom were "booed and heckled" during attempts to deliver campaign speeches. A political ally of the administration cautioned Clifford that "something should be done to lessen the tension over this situation in New York City, if the Democratic party is to get anywhere in the coming elections in the state." [20]

Discouraged by the contradiction between the secretary of state's comments and the Democratic platform's plank, the Zionists asked Truman to clear away the uncertainty by stating exactly where the administration stood on the issue of Israel's boundaries.[21] Yet Truman still was opposed to making any such statement. Once the campaign was under way, it was generally agreed that the candidates were bound to respect an informal understanding not to make political issues out of American foreign policy. By modifying or repudiating Marshall's statement, the president might have opened himself to the charge of making a political issue of the Israeli situation.

Republicans were able to take advantage of Truman's dilemma. John Foster Dulles, a member of the American mission to the United Nations and the man acknowledged to be Dewey's choice for secretary of state, withheld his support from Marshall's acceptance of the Bernadotte plan. Dulles's refusal to back Marshall was viewed as an indication that Dewey disapproved of the terms included in Bernadotte's report. This was such an indirect repudiation, however, that the Democrats did not believe they could charge a violation of the bipartisan "agreement" on foreign policy.[22] Although Democrats and Republicans alike claimed they were guided by the principle of bipartisanship, it was left unclear by both sides just how restrictive they meant their pledges to be in 1948.

DEWEY'S REMARKS
SPARK A PRESIDENTIAL REPLY

On October 22, Dewey gave Truman an opportunity to fight back in regard to the Bernadotte plan. In a publicly released letter to Dean Alfange, chairman of the American Palestine Committee of New York, Dewey attacked the administration's vacillation concerning Israel's boundaries. Although not specifically referring to the Bernadotte proposal to remove the Negev from the Jewish state, the Republican nominee emphasized that he was still supporting the boundaries for Israel that were designated in the United Nations partition resolution.[23]

This was not as direct a violation of the bipartisanship principle as the Democrats later charged, but it was all Clifford needed. He was suddenly given the ammunition that enabled him to persuade the president to adopt a course of action that Clifford had been recommending for months. On October 23, after learning of Dewey's remarks, Clifford spent most of the morning with Lovett. In a memorandum to the president that same day, Clifford noted: "I explained to Lovett [that] your integrity has been attacked by Dewey, whose purpose is to infer that you have reneged on [the] Democratic Platform." Clifford told Lovett that Truman "would have to give out [a] statement clearly stating [his] position on Israel. Lovett agrees." Following his lengthy session with Clifford, Lovett "sent Marshall a cable stating in substance that Dewey had violated [the] bi-partisan approach on Israel and that Lovett feels that [the] President has to reaffirm his support of [the]

Democratic Platform." Clifford explained to Truman that he was "working on a statement on Israel now" and would have it ready for the president's consideration by the next day. Ending the memorandum on an optimistic note, Clifford wrote: "I consider Dewey's action a serious error on his part and the best thing that has happened to us to date." [24]

Truman approved Clifford's draft, and the presidential remarks were released on October 24. Reflecting the hope of recapturing any lost support among Jews, the statement was a calculated political pronouncement. In the text, Clifford included the advocacy of policies that he had been sponsoring. "I had hoped," the president's statement solemnly began, "our foreign affairs could continue to be handled on a non-partisan basis without being injected into the presidential campaign. The Republican candidate's statement, however, makes it necessary for me to reiterate my own position with respect to Palestine." Truman stressed that he stood "squarely on the provisions covering Israel in the Democratic Platform." Since the Democratic platform endorsed the boundaries of the partition resolution and opposed any geographical revision without Israeli approval, the president's announcement was at odds with the secretary of state's public stance. Marshall had asked for the acceptance of the Bernadotte plan "in its entirety," asserting that it offered "a generally fair basis for settlement of the Palestine question." Truman, on the other hand, minimized the significance of the plan, noting only that it did offer "a basis of negotiation." Truman also pointed out that he had already ordered the appropriate agencies to arrange for a loan to Israel and he hoped it would be granted soon. Moreover, following the election of a permanent government in Israel, Truman pledged, "it will promptly be given *de jure* recognition." [25]

Accepting the argument that, thanks to Dewey's comments, it was now possible for him to open up on the Israel issue, Truman delivered the strongest pro-Israel declaration of the campaign on October 28 at Madison Square Garden in New

York City. Supporters of the Jewish state were left with no doubts regarding the president's intention to develop a close relationship with Israel. Ignoring any direct reference to the Bernadotte plan, Truman told his audience that Israel "must be large enough, free enough and strong enough to make its people self-supporting and secure." Whereas he had merely modified the American enthusiasm for the Bernadotte plan in his October 24 statement, he now in effect repudiated it. "I had stood," the president announced, "and still stand, on the present Democratic platform of 1948."

Applauding the Israeli experiment, Truman went on to say that "what we need now is to help the people of Israel, and they've proved themselves in the best tradition of hardy pioneers. They have created out of a barren desert a modern and efficient state with the highest standards of western civilization." Truman also recalled his own version of the administration's contribution to the establishment of the Jewish state. Under his leadership, the United States was "responsible" for the United Nations partition resolution, as well as being the first country to grant recognition to Israel. "I have never changed my position on Palestine or Israel," Truman emphatically declared to a receptive throng of some sixteen thousand persons.

In this out-and-out political address, Truman contradicted the record, public and private, when he went on to contend that the Israeli issue "must not be resolved as a matter of politics during a political campaign. I've refused consistently to play politics with that subject." Finally, he agreed to help Israel "take its place in the family of nations. . . . [However,] we'll not work toward it in a partisan or political way." [26]

Truman delivered his Madison Square Garden speech just six days before the election. Political opponents immediately charged the president with exploiting the Israeli issue for political gain. Henry Wallace, for example, responded to Truman's statement by saying that the president was unsuccessfully attempting to cleanse his hands of the blood of Israel [27] and Republican United States Senator Irving Ives commented that Truman "has run out on every commitment he has ever made to the Jewish people." [28] The evidence is overwhelming, not only in the official statements but also in the record of behind-the-scenes maneuverings, that the president was deliberately and calculatingly playing politics with this explosive issue.

12

The Jewish Vote
and the Aftermath of the Election

TRUMAN WINS REELECTION

Democratic efforts to capture New York State in the presidential election fell just short of success. Out of more than 6,100,000 ballots cast in the state, Dewey's plurality was only 60,959, or less than 1 percent of the total vote. Since Truman had to campaign against both Dewey, a popular governor, and Henry Wallace, a third-party candidate, he started with a difficult handicap. Wallace, with his progressive political stance, attracted many New Yorkers who would doubtless have voted for the president if limited to a choice between Truman and Dewey; indeed, he received nearly one-half of his nationwide total of 1,157,000 votes in New York State.

Included among the 422,000 Wallace voters in New York City were large numbers of Jews who normally backed the Democrats. It is difficult to ascertain how much of Wallace's strength among Jews was based on his consistent pro-Zionist position; it is probable that most Jewish voters for Wallace were expressing general approval of his progressive political views.[1] But even taking into account the Jewish defections to Wallace, it appears that Truman received between 60 and 75 percent of the nationwide Jewish vote, whereas estimates are that Dewey was held to 10 to 20 percent.[2]

Losing New York State to Dewey did not prove fatal to the president's reelection bid. In one of the more stunning upsets in American political history, Truman outdistanced Dewey

303–189 in the electoral college, thus becoming the first candidate since Woodrow Wilson to lose New York but win the
presidency. The double irony is that for all his desperate striv-
ing to win New York by an appeal to the Jewish vote, Truman did not carry the state, and yet as events turned out he
did not need it to win.

It is entirely possible, however, that Truman's emphatic
shift to a pro-Zionist stance in the closing stages of the campaign was, after all, one of the key factors in his victory. It is
probable that many votes that were slipping away to Wallace or
Dewey were salvaged when Truman finally came out again
four-square for Israel. This hypothesis is strengthened in view
of the fact that a switch from Truman to Dewey of 29,294
votes in three key states—Ohio, California, and Illinois—
would have made Dewey president. Although a small shift of
any group might have been equally significant, the importance
of Jewish voters in these particular states cannot be overlooked. Each had a large Jewish community, and Jews notably vote in proportions "far in excess of the national
average." [3] The following figures for these three states, each of
which Truman carried, illustrate the hypothesis:

State	Electoral Votes in 1948	Shift from Truman to Dewey Necessary for Dewey to Carry State	Estimated Jewish Population (Including Minors)
Ohio	25	3,554	143,000
California	25	8,933	358,000
Illinois	28	16,807	340,000

By winning these three states, Dewey would have reversed
the electoral count to 267–225 in his favor. It would appear
that Truman did attract at least 29,194 last-minute votes from
among the 841,000 Jews in Ohio, California, and Illinois as a
result of the Israeli policy he proposed late in the campaign.
A switch from Truman to Dewey of only 12,487 votes in

Ohio and California—or 0.03 percent of the 46,075,034 ballots cast for Truman and Dewey—would have prevented either candidate from attaining victory. Although Truman would have led 253–239 in such an event, the thirty-nine electoral votes that States' Rights nominee J. Strom Thurmond collected in the South would have made a decision by the House of Representatives necessary.[4]

Had Truman been unable to prevent the traditionally Democratic voters from deserting en masse to the Wallace camp, the same electoral turnabout would have resulted. However, twice as many defections from Truman to Wallace would have been required for Dewey to have won or for the election to have been thrown into the House of Representatives. It is difficult to evaluate the manner in which Dewey and Wallace would have split the ballots that were ultimately denied them as a result of the president's last-minute dramatic appeal to Jewish voters.

Shortly after the election, Truman honored his campaign commitments regarding Israel. On January 19, 1949, the White House announced the authorization of a loan of one hundred million dollars to Israel.[5] Elections for a permanent Israeli government were held on January 25; six days later the United States extended de jure, or full, recognition to Israel.[6] Pledges both to grant a loan and to extend de jure recognition had been included in Truman's statement of October 24, 1948.[7]

Since the establishment of Israel, a popular myth has existed that perpetuates the claim that Truman had been an unswerving supporter of Jewish designs in the Middle East. When the chief rabbi of Israel was received at the White House in 1949, for example, he is reported to have told the president, "God put you in your mother's womb so you would be the instrument to bring about the rebirth of Israel after two thousand years."[8] Edward Jacobson insisted that Truman "should be daily blessed in every synagogue and every temple the world over."[9] One Jewish group, in an effort to show its appreciation to the president, decided to establish a 50,000–tree Harry S. Truman Forest in Israel.[10]

THE ARAB-ISRAELI
AGREEMENT TO END HOSTILITIES

Efforts to bring peace to the Middle East continued throughout 1949. The second truce agreement (see p. 116), which had gone into effect on July 18, 1948, was shattered in mid-October when the Egyptians renewed the conflict. Subsequent fighting resulted in continued success for the Israelis. Stung by military reverses, the Egyptian government notified the United Nations mediator, Ralph Bunche, that it was ready to negotiate with Israel under United Nations sponsorship. Fighting ceased on January 7, 1949, and five days later the official discussions began at Rhodes.[11]

Bunche, who displayed brilliant diplomatic skill during the talks, insisted upon a policy of separate negotiations between Israel and each of the Arab states that had agreed to work for a settlement. On February 24, 1949, representatives of the Egyptian and Israeli governments signed a general armistice agreement. Similar arrangements between the Jewish state and Lebanon, Jordan, and Syria were concluded shortly thereafter. Since armistice demarcation lines were determined approximately in accordance with the territory held under the military control of each country, the 1949 settlement left Israel one-fourth larger than she would have been had partition been implemented.[12] With the armistice negotiations concluded, an uneasy peace settled over the Holy Land.

— 13 —

Truman's Policy in Retrospect

It will be remembered that Truman adopted a cautious approach toward the Zionists during his first months in the White House. Following a period of hesitation, he endorsed, on August 31, 1945, a Zionist proposal that called on Great Britain to open Palestine immediately to the immigration of one hundred thousand Jewish refugees. While London was aroused by what it considered to be an inappropriate demand by the United States, the Zionists were disappointed that the president had embraced only one aspect of their program for Palestine. When Britain requested that an Anglo–American inquiry be made to review the whole Palestine question, Truman agreed to the plan although he was reluctant about delaying any longer the admission of Jews into Palestine. In the spring of 1946 the report of the Anglo–American Committee of Inquiry recommended that Great Britain prepare for the immediate evacuation of one hundred thousand Jewish refugees from Europe into Palestine. Within a few weeks, however, London flatly rejected the proposal.

By the fall of 1946, Truman's Palestine policy had alienated the British, the Jews, and the Arabs. Great Britain was annoyed at the American demand that Palestine be opened to refugees, the Arabs bitterly opposed the United States endorsement of any part of the Zionist program, and the Jews were angered because Truman had not used the full power of his office to pressure the British government into accepting the American request.

With his political support among Jews waning, Truman was

persuaded, in large measure by David Niles, an administrative assistant, to counter apparent Republican inroads among Jewish voters by endorsing the most crucial part of the Zionist program. Accordingly, on October 4, 1946, just one month before the congressional elections, Truman called for the establishment of a Jewish state in Palestine. The president's statement was issued on Yom Kippur, the most sacred day in the Hebrew religious calendar.

Early in 1947, Britain asked the United Nations to summon a special session of the General Assembly to recommend a solution to the Palestine problem. Since Truman had already endorsed the establishment of a Jewish state in Palestine, the Zionists were hoping the United States would lead the campaign for that cause during the United Nations debate. The president, however, now insisted upon an American policy of complete neutrality while a special United Nations committee debated the future government of Palestine.

On August 31, 1947, the special committee issued a report for the General Assembly to consider. A majority of the committee members recommended a partition of Palestine into two independent states, one Jewish and the other Arab. When Truman backed the partition plan in the fall of 1947, it seemed the only solution then being considered by the General Assembly that was worthy of American support. During the General Assembly debate on the partition plan, the United States delegation proselytized for its adoption to a very limited degree. Although restrained, the American contribution helped to secure a narrow passage for the partition proposal on November 29, 1947.

Early in 1948, Truman began to back away from his previous endorsement of partition. With the sudden worsening of East–West relations, the president found those proposals appealing which were designed to postpone any showdown in Palestine. Persuaded by his advisers in the State Department that an attempt to implement partition would be harmful to the national security, Truman agreed to a reversal of the

American policy favoring implementation. During the first two weeks in March the State Department made preparations to announce the shift in policy to the United Nations. On March 19, the American ambassador to the United Nations, Warren Austin, told the Security Council that the United States believed the partition plan should be set aside indefinitely. Austin proposed that the United Nations administer Palestine through a temporary trusteeship. Assurances from the State Department that the United Nations would adopt the trusteeship scheme proved to be misleading; officials within the department had badly misjudged the potential for support among member nations.

Not only was the State Department trusteeship plan unable to stop a full-scale civil war from erupting in Palestine once the British mandate expired on May 15, 1948, but the reversal brought domestic political consequences that were difficult for Truman to ignore. Clark Clifford, special counsel to the president, had emphasized to Truman the necessity for Democrats to secure widespread political support within the American Jewish community. Shortly before May 15, the Zionists confirmed their intention of establishing a state once the mandate ended. During a White House conference on Palestine, convened on May 12, Clifford argued that the president, with a national election less than six months away, should move toward redeeming himself with Jewish voters by immediately recognizing the existence of the Jewish state. Truman extended de facto American recognition to Israel just eleven minutes after the expiration of the British mandate.

For three years Truman's decisions on Palestine had vacillated according to the changing pressures of the moment. Holding no firm convictions regarding Zionist goals in Palestine, he found himself in the middle of a virtual tug-of-war on the issue. Representatives of the State Department, the Department of Defense, and the military advised against adoption of a pro-Zionist policy which, they claimed, would militate against the American national interest by alienating the

Arabs. In opposition to these officials were members of the president's personal staff who urged bold sponsorship of the Zionist program in the Middle East.

In the spring of 1948, those who favored Truman's endorsement of a pro-Zionist policy finally triumphed. Most notable among the victors was Clifford, who had contended that the winning political strategy for the Democrats in 1948 must include solid Jewish support. Beginning with his precipitate recognition of the state of Israel on May 14, the president embarked on a politically expedient course designed to win the favor of the American Jewish community. Truman's appeals to the Jewish voters, who were overwhelmingly pro-Zionist, culminated a few days before the election with a statement and speech promising extensive American support for Israel.

Although since 1948 Truman has been lauded for his contribution to the creation of Israel, much of the adulation has been misplaced. The president had no commitment to the Zionist program. When he abandoned the United Nations partition plan in March 1948 and dealt what some observers believed would be the death blow to any hope for a Jewish state, he was acting out of consideration for the exigencies of national security. Similarly, when his policies were in accord with the Zionists' program, he was motivated primarily, if not solely, by political exigencies. With all its contradictions and vacillations, Truman's Palestine-Israel policy offers an extraordinary example of foreign policy conducted in line with short-range political expediency rather than long-range national goals.

Notes

INTRODUCTION

1. Numerous examples can be cited of a president capitulating to popular demands. For instance, an aroused citizenry forced President Grover Cleveland in 1893 to abandon plans to restore Queen Liliuokalani to her Hawaiian throne. In 1921 popular clamor resulted in the convening of the Washington Disarmament Conference during Warren Harding's administration; and in 1928 Calvin Coolidge was similarly compelled to negotiate the antiwar Kellogg-Briand pact (although reluctant to involve himself in the proceedings, Secretary of State Frank Kellogg won a Nobel Peace Prize for his efforts). In the mid-1930s the Franklin Roosevelt administration, despite its opposition to noninterventionist legislation, bowed to public pressure and supported a series of Neutrality Acts intended to insure American isolation from foreign embroilments. Thomas A. Bailey, *A Diplomatic History of the American People,* 8th ed. (New York, 1969), chap. 1; Thomas A. Bailey, *The Man in the Street: The Impact of American Public Opinion on Foreign Policy* (New York, 1948), pp. 1–11.

2. Bailey, *Man in the Street,* p. 14; Louis Gerson, *The Hyphenate in Recent American Politics and Diplomacy* (Lawrence, Kans., 1964), pp. xiii, 3, 6, 284.

3. Gerson, *Hyphenate in . . . Politics,* pp. 6, 29, 30.

4. Lawrence H. Fuchs, "Minority Groups and Foreign Policy," *Political Science Quarterly* 76 (June 1959): 162, 164–65; Gerson, *Hyphenate in . . . Politics,* p. 250; Bailey, *Man in the Street,* p. 2.

5. Bailey, *Diplomatic History,* p. 510.

141

6. Fuchs, "Minority Groups," p. 171; Bailey, *Man in the Street,* pp. 15, 17, 88; Gerson, *Hyphenate in . . . Politics,* p. 11.

1: ORGANIZING FOR A JEWISH STATE

1. The word "Zionism" derives from "Zion," one of the hills upon which ancient Jerusalem was built. Anny Latour, *The Resurrection of Israel,* trans. Margaret S. Summers (Cleveland, n.d.), p. 8. For material on the early history of Zionism, see Alan R. Taylor, *Prelude to Israel: An Analysis of Zionist Diplomacy, 1897–1947* (New York, 1949); Sumner Welles, *We Need Not Fail* (Boston, 1948); and Richard H. S. Crossman, *A Nation Reborn* (New York, 1960).

2. Leonard Stein, *The Balfour Declaration* (New York, 1961), p. 550; Ronald Sanders, *Israel: The View from Masada* (New York, 1964), pp. 25, 117, 121.

3. Howard Sachar, *The Emergence of the Middle East: 1914–1924* (New York, 1969), p. 212; Selig Adler, "The Palestine Question in the Wilson Era," *Jewish Social Studies* 10 (October 1948): 305–8, 334; Stein, *Balfour Declaration,* pp. 196, 503–5, 597–600.

4. It is not known which of Brandeis's arguments were responsible for Wilson's shift. Adler, "Palestine Question in the Wilson Era," p. 307; Stein, *Balfour Declaration,* pp. 195, 197, 508–10; Sachar, *Emergence of the Middle East,* p. 213. Selig Adler and Leonard Stein, the two historians who have written the most thorough accounts of this episode, are convinced that it was Brandeis's persuasiveness which was responsible for changing the president's mind.

5. Sachar, *Emergence of the Middle East,* p. 213; Stein, *Balfour Declaration,* pp. 196–97.

6. Esco Foundation for Palestine, *Palestine: A Study of Jewish, Arab and British Policies,* 2 vols. (New Haven, 1947), 1:107.

7. Stein, *Balfour Declaration,* pp. 552–53.

8. United Nations, General Assembly, *Official Records,* Second Session, "United Nations Special Committee on Palestine," Annex 19 (A/364), 1947, pp. 18–21.

9. *Ibid.,* chap. 2, p. 23.

10. Phillip S. Bernstein, "Palestine and the Jew—A Reply," *Christian Century,* February 4, 1948, p. 138; *New York Times,* November 3, 1945, p. 2; July 31, 1945, p. 11; February 7, 1947, p. 8.

11. According to Roper, 80.1 percent of those Jews questioned agreed that the establishment of a Jewish state would be "a good thing for the Jews"; 10.5 percent said a Jewish state "would be bad for the Jews"; and 9.4 percent were undecided. Elmo Roper, *A Survey of American Jewish Opinion* (New York, October 1945), pp. 1–10.

12. Samuel Halperin, *The Political World of American Zionism* (Detroit, 1961), p. 327.

13. *Ibid.,* pp. 270–73. It is impossible to uncover the total expenditure since, in addition to the national budget, enormous sums were raised and spent locally. In Philadelphia, for example, local Zionists raised $50,000 from $100–a–plate dinners to help finance a campaign against the British white paper.

14. Memorandum, Andie Knutson to Philleo Nash, August 6, 1951, tables 2 and 5, Nash Files, Truman Library, Independence, Mo. (cited hereafter as Nash Files).

15. Memorandum, Andie Knutson to Philleo Nash, July 24, 1951, table 5, Nash Files.

16. A copy of this handbill was found in "Palestine Analysis," folder 2, Nash Files.

17. The mandate for Palestine that Britain received in 1922 from the League of Nations provided for "an appropriate Jewish Agency." The agency was to cooperate with the Palestinian government in establishing a Jewish national home and also to assist in developing the country. At the outset the World Zionist Organization itself fulfilled the role of the agency. In 1929, however, a separate Jewish Agency for Palestine was created. The ruling body of the organization was the twenty-member Executive. By the late 1940s the Jewish Agency functioned in effect as a shadow government for a Jewish state that Zionists hoped to establish in Palestine. *New York Times,* May 11, 1947, sec. 4, p. 5.

18. Leonard Slater, *The Pledge* (New York, 1970), pp. 83,

127, 168, 308. Slater's book is an engaging account of the contribution that Americans made to assist the emerging state of Israel. Although overall it is a credible source, it should be noted that Slater's research involved personal interviews with participants years after the events took place. Caution should be used in evaluating some of the specific details.

19. *Ibid.,* pp. 21, 35, 40, 78, 131, 255.

20. *Ibid.,* pp. 3–7, 49–50, 53, 151–63.

21. *Ibid.,* pp. 282, 286–300.

22. *Ibid.,* p. 321.

23. Halperin, *Political World of American Zionism,* pp. 284, 291.

24. Gerson, *Hyphenate in . . . Politics,* p. 154. Also see H. Bradford Westerfield, *Foreign Policy and Party Politics* (New Haven, 1955), p. 227.

25. An American Institute of Public Opinion (AIPO) poll of June 19, 1946, showed that 78 percent felt it was a good idea to admit a hundred thousand Jews into Palestine, 14 percent thought it was a bad idea, and 8 percent had no opinion. An AIPO poll of December 5, 1945, found 76 percent in favor of permitting Jews to enter Palestine and only 7 percent opposed. When polled on its opinion of establishing a Jewish state in Palestine, the public recorded its narrowest margin of support in a survey taken in December, 1944, by the National Opinion Research Center (NORC). The survey found 36 percent in favor of a Jewish state, 32 percent against, and 32 percent uncommitted. However, another NORC poll, taken in February, 1948, showed 38 percent supporting statehood, 19 percent against, and 15 percent undecided; 28 percent said they were unfamiliar with the subject. The AIPO poll of November 19, 1947, which asked the same question, indicated 65 percent in favor, 10 percent opposed; 25 percent had no opinion. *Public Opinion Quarterly* 10 (Fall, 1946): 161, 418, 550; Hadley Cantril, ed., *Public Opinion: 1935–1946* (Princeton, 1951), pp. 385–86.

26. See the NORC poll of May 1946, and the AIPO survey of September 11, 1946. Cantril, *Public Opinion,* pp. 385, 387.

2: TRUMAN SEEKS A POLICY

1. Abba Eban to President Harry S. Truman, January 10, 1952, Official File 204-D, Truman Papers, Truman Library, Independence, Mo. (cited hereafter as Truman Papers).

2. 'John C. Campbell, *Defense of the Middle East* (New York, 1960), p. 31; Cordell Hull, *Memoirs of Cordell Hull,* 2 vols. (New York, 1948), 2:1517–18; Frank Manuel, *The Realities of American-Palestine Relations* (Washington, D.C., 1949), pp. 334–42; Nadav Safran, *The United States and Israel* (Cambridge, Mass., 1963), p. 37.

3. For further background on this subject, see Loy W. Henderson, "American Political and Strategic Interest in the Middle East and Southeastern Europe," *Department of State Bulletin,* November 23, 1947, pp. 996–1000.

4. Walter Millis, ed., *The Forrestal Diaries* (New York, 1951), p. 323. Also see Sidney B. Fay, "Oil and the Middle East," *Current History* 8 (April 1945): 339.

5. *Platt's Oilgram News Service,* July 19, 1971, p. 1; Walter Levy, "Oil Power," *Foreign Affairs* 49 (July 1971): 652.

6. Campbell, *Defense of the Middle East,* p. 250; *Platt's Oilgram News Service,* July 19, 1971, p. 1.

7. Campbell, *Defense of the Middle East,* pp. 250–52; Kermit Roosevelt, "The Partition of Palestine: A Lesson in Pressure Politics," *Middle East Journal* 2 (January 1948): 9; *New York Times,* May 15, 1947, p. 12; February 13, 1948, p. 16.

8. According to *New York Times* Middle East correspondent Clifton Daniel, one example of such threats of economic sanctions against the United States occurred in late 1945 when the Lebanese parliament failed to accept a proposal to build two refineries, to be financed in part by two American companies, in Lebanon. Daniel also reported on a 1946 conference in Syria attended by representatives of seven Arab states. The resolutions agreed upon, although not made public, were generally thought to include potential economic sanctions against the United States if American policy became too sympathetic toward the Zionists. *New York Times,* October 25, 1945, p. 1; September 28, 1947, sec. 4, p. 4.

9. Manuel, *American-Palestine Relations,* p. 335.

10. Campbell, *Defense of the Middle East,* pp. 167, 175; *New York Times,* February 13, 1948, p. 16.

11. Campbell, *Defense of the Middle East,* pp. 4, 16.

12. *The Common Purpose of Civilized Mankind* (New York, 1942), pp. 4–6; *Congressional Record,* 76th Cong., 1st sess., 1939, p. A2231.

13. In resigning from the committee, Truman said that "it is certainly outside my policy to be mixed up in such an organization." Harry S. Truman to Stephen Wise, June 1, 1943, Robert Wagner Papers, Georgetown University, Washington, D.C. (cited hereafter as Wagner Papers). Also see Abram S. Magida to Philip Levy (secretary to Senator Wagner), June 3, 1943, Wagner Papers. Magida, an employee of the committee, verified that Truman had been a member of the Committee for a Jewish Army, an organization strongly committed to Zionist goals, until the newspaper advertisement in question prompted his resignation.

14. Draft by Senator Truman, "Statement for American Zionist Emergency Council," May 1944, General File (Jews), Truman Papers. Emphasis added.

15. Harry S. Truman, *Memoirs,* vol. 2, *Years of Trial and Hope* (Garden City, N.Y., 1956), p. 133.

16. Roosevelt to Robert Wagner, co-chairman, American Palestine Committee, May 23, 1942, Wagner Papers. Wagner inserted the letter into the *Congressional Record.*

17. Memorandum, Joseph C. Grew, acting secretary of state, to Truman, May 14, 1945, OF 204–Misc., Truman Papers. Grew wrote the memorandum to inform Truman of a series of letters Roosevelt had sent to Arab leaders in response to their inquiries concerning American policy toward Palestine.

18. Truman, *Memoirs,* 2:134.

19. Truman to Amir Abd Allah Ibn Husain (later King Abdullah of Jordan), May 17, 1945, OF 204–Misc., Truman Papers.

20. Truman, *Memoirs,* 2:164.

21. *Public Papers of the Presidents of the United States, 1945* (Washington, D.C., 1961), p. 228.

22. Truman, *Memoirs,* 2:137.

23. *New York Times,* September 30, 1945, p. 38.

24. Truman, *Memoirs,* 2:136–37, 140.

25. Truman to Attlee, August 31, 1945, OF 204-Misc., Truman Papers.

26. *Ibid.*

27. On September 23, for example, the American Zionist Emergency Council urged the administration to give its full support to the Zionist program. Six days later Joseph Proskauer and Jacob Blaustein, the president and chairman, respectively, of the Executive Committee of the American Jewish Committee, met with Truman to ask him to use his office to effect a substantial increase in Jewish immigration to Palestine. *New York Times,* September 24, 1945, p. 1; September 30, 1945, p. 39.

28. Rabbi Silver to Senator Robert Wagner, September 6, 1945, Wagner Papers.

29. *New York Times,* September 24, 1945, p. 1.

30. Truman to Virginia Gildersleeve, October 15, 1945, OF 204-Misc., Truman Papers.

31. The spokesman quoted here was Abd al-Rahman Azzam Bey, secretary-general of the Arab League. *New York Times,* August 20, 1945, p. 17; October 5, 1945, p. 2.

32. *Public Papers of the Presidents . . . , 1945,* p. 347.

33. According to Daniel, ibn-Saud had been annoyed by Washington's denial that any letter existed and had been threatening to release the correspondence for some time. *New York Times,* October 20, 1945, p. 5.

34. Truman, *Memoirs,* 2:140.

35. Roosevelt to ibn-Saud, April 5, 1945, Weizmann Archives, Truman Library (cited hereafter as Weizmann Archives).

36. Herbert Feis, *The Birth of Israel: The Tousled Diplomatic Bed* (New York, 1969), p. 16.

37. Memorandum, American Zionist Emergency Council to the State Department, October 23, 1945, OF 204-Misc., Truman Papers.

38. *Ibid.*

39. Rabbi Wise and Rabbi Abba Hillel Silver, co-chairmen of the American Zionist Emergency Council, met with Secretary of

State Byrnes and argued that the government should not be "intimidated or blackmailed" into retreating from its earlier support of the Zionist program. Hadassah, the largest women's Zionist organization in the United States, passed a resolution at its national convention expressing its "sense of shock" that the American Government would not repudiate the suggestion that it was not committed to supporting the Zionist goals. Failure to disavow the claim that the United States was not in favor of establishing a Jewish state "disregarded the fact that the American Government already has a positive policy with regard to Palestine." *New York Times,* October 23, 1945, p. 4; October 24, 1945, p. 12.

40. Truman, *Memoirs,* 2:140.

41. Truman to Abdullah, no date given (presumably October 1945), OF 204-Misc., Truman Papers. Also see telegram, Abdullah to Truman, September 29, 1945, OF 204-Misc., Truman Papers.

42. Truman, *Memoirs,* 2:141–42.

43. Richard Crossman, one of the six British members of the Anglo-American Committee of Inquiry, makes this argument. Crossman, *A Nation Reborn,* p. 3. Wise and Silver, co-chairmen of the American Zionist Emergency Council, made the same assessment when they learned of the committee's formation. *New York Times,* November 15, 1945, p. 4.

44. *New York Times,* November 15, 1945, p. 4. Additional Zionist criticism of the committee is available in the following material: Telegram, Stephen Wise and Abba Hillel Silver to Truman, November 15, 1945, OF 204-Misc., Truman Papers; Emanuel Celler to Truman, November 15, 1945, OF 204-Misc., Truman Papers; *New York Times,* November 19, 1945, p. 8.

45. Truman, *Memoirs,* 2:143.

46. On December 10, 1945, Truman named the following persons to the American delegation: Joseph C. Hutcheson (chairman), Frank Aydelotte, Frank Buxton, O. Max Gardner, James G. McDonald, and William Phillips. *New York Times,* October 11, 1945, p. 1; *Public Papers of the Presidents . . . , 1945,* pp. 531–33. When Gardner declined to serve, Truman replaced him with Bartley C. Crum, *New York Times,* December 19, 1945, p. 14.

47. Bartley C. Crum, *Behind the Silken Curtain* (New York, 1947), pp. 8, 36–38, 40.

48. David B. Sachar, "David K. Niles and United States Policy toward Palestine," unpublished undergraduate honors thesis (Harvard University, 1959), p. 22. Sachar quotes a memorandum, Niles to Loy Henderson, no date given, that is among the Niles papers at Brandeis University. Sachar was granted access to the Niles papers for his use in writing his thesis. Other researchers, including the author, have had their requests to examine the Niles papers refused by Sachar's father, Abram L. Sachar. The elder Sachar, a close friend of Niles, has served as both president and chancellor of Brandeis University.

49. *Ibid.* Sachar's evidence is based on a memorandum, Niles to Crum, no date given, that he located among the Niles papers.

50. *Ibid.,* p. 26. Britain sought and received a ten-day delay to allow cabinet consideration before the report was publicly announced. Sachar cites a telegram, British Foreign Office to Lord Halifax, date not given, that is included among the Niles papers.

51. *New York Times,* March 1, 1946, p. 15.

52. *Ibid.,* December 13, 1945, p. 10.

53. Memorandum, Roberta Barrows (a White House secretary) to Truman, October 24, 1945, OF 204-Misc., Truman Papers.

54. *Public Papers of the Presidents . . . , 1945,* p. 509.

55. Truman to Wagner, December 10, 1945, Wagner Papers.

56. *New York Times,* December 13, 1945, p. 10.

57. *Ibid.*

58. *Ibid.,* December 18, 1945, p. 1.

59. *Congressional Record,* 79th Cong., 1st sess., 1945, p. 12396.

60. Halperin, *Political World of American Zionism,* p. 273.

3: BRITISH AND ARAB RESISTANCE

1. *New York Times,* May 9, 1946, p. 9.

2. *Ibid.,* May 1, 1946, p. 13. This quotation is from Jamal el Husseini, chairman of the Arab Higher Committee. According to

a cable from another Arab leader, "The Whole Iraq Nation condemn the recommendations of the Anglo-American Committee." Telegram, Muhammad Hasan Kubbah, president, Chamber of Deputies, Iraq, to Truman, May 6, 1946, OF 204-B, Truman Papers. One Arab spokesman informed the American president that the committee report had caused "great anxiety and deep disappointment throughout the Arab world." Telegram, Abd al-Ilah, regent and heir apparent, Iraq, to Truman, May 9, 1946, OF 204-B, Truman Papers. The heads of diplomatic missions representing five Arab states (Egypt, Iraq, Lebanon, Saudi Arabia, and Syria) issued a statement declaring that any attempt to implement the committee recommendation regarding Jewish immigration would be resisted with whatever force the Arabs should find necessary. *New York Times*, May 3, 1946, p. 3.

3. The American Zionist Emergency Council, representing Zionist organizations with six hundred thousand enrolled members, announced on May 1 its enthusiasm for the recommendation to admit one hundred thousand Jews into Palestine, but the failure of the report to support the creation of a Jewish state received the council's censure. *New York Times*, May 2, 1946, p. 2. The Jewish Agency for Palestine also welcomed the decision regarding one hundred thousand refugees, but it failed to endorse the report since "the central problem of the homeless, stateless Jewish people has been left untouched" by the Anglo-American committee. *Ibid.*, May 1, 1946, p. 1.

4. Jewish Agency for Palestine to Truman, May 2, 1946, OF 204-Misc., Truman Papers.

5. *Public Papers of the Presidents of the United States, 1946* (Washington, D.C., 1962), pp. 218–19.

6. Truman, *Memoirs*, 2:146–47; Feis, *Birth of Israel*, p. 28.

7. *New York Times*, May 2, 1945, p. 1.

8. Truman, *Memoirs*, 2:149.

9. *Ibid.*, p. 150.

10. On May 2, 1946, six American members of the Executive of the Jewish Agency for Palestine (Silver, Wise, Nahum Goldman, Louis Lipsky, Eliahu Epstein, and Meyer Weisgal) expressed their "profoundest satisfaction" to the president for his efforts in behalf of opening Palestine to one hundred thousand refugees. Ex-

ecutive of the Jewish Agency to Truman, May 2, 1946, OF 204-Misc., Truman Papers. Edmund Kaufmann, a former president of the Zionist Organization of America, wrote to Truman on May 8 to offer his appreciation. "No one," wrote Kaufmann, "knows better than I the profound influence that you exerted in order that this act of justice might be initiated." Kaufmann to Truman, May 8, 1946, OF 204-Misc., Truman Papers. As the AZEC statement by Wise and Silver indicates, by early June the Zionist spokesmen were far less enthusiastic. *New York Times,* June 5, 1946, p. 8.

11. *Public Papers of the Presidents . . . , 1946,* p. 287. According to United Press International coverage of the news conference, Truman's statement had been "prodded by an angry Senate clamor for the immediate admission of 100,000" Jews to Palestine. The president's comments "came after heated Senate debate in which the British Government was severely criticized for stalling." Although several senators spoke out in strong terms against further delay, Colorado's Edwin C. Johnson was the most critical. Johnson said that Hitler was receiving "magnificent assistance" in his extermination of Jews from "an autocratic, straight-laced British Colonial Office." *New York Times,* June 7, 1946, p. 11.

12. *New York Times,* June 13, 1946, p. 1.

13. The Arab Higher Committee, the internationally recognized representative agency of the Palestinian Arabs, notified the British cabinet that if the report were implemented, "the Arabs will proceed to organize national forces and prepare all means for defense in order to resume the national struggle." *Ibid.,* May 3, 1946, p. 3. The Arab League was an organization established by seven Arab states in part to develop a common policy in opposition to the Zionist program for Palestine. On May 16, 1946, five of the member states of the Arab League (Egypt, Iraq, Lebanon, Saudi Arabia, and Syria) presented an aide-mémoire to the United States government which said that American support of the Anglo-American committee recommendations would be considered "hostile to the Arab people," and would "result in a state of disturbance and conflict in Palestine and in the Near and Middle East, and would be harmful to security and peace in that strategic part of the world." *Ibid.,* May 17, 1946, p. 1. Iraq's House of Representatives unanimously adopted a resolution which insisted that the committee report "inevitably will lead to disturbances of

the peace and security of the Middle East" if attempts were to be made to carry them out. *Ibid.,* May 8, 1946, p. 2.

14. *Ibid.,* June 13, 1946, pp. 1, 4.

15. *Public Papers of the Presidents . . . , 1946,* p. 297.

16. *New York Times,* June 30, 1946, p. 30; July 2, 1946, p. 1.

17. Matthew J. Connelly, secretary to the president, to the Jewish Agency for Palestine, July 18, 1946, OF 204-Misc., Truman Papers. Although the letter was sent over Connelly's signature, it was actually drafted by David Niles (memorandum, Truman to Niles, July 10, 1946, OF 204-Misc., Truman Papers).

18. *New York Times,* July 26, 1946, p. 1.

19. *Ibid.*

20. *Ibid.,* August 8, 1946, p. 11.

21. *Ibid.,* August 4, 1946, p. 1.

22. *Ibid.,* July 27, 1946, p. 6; August 6, 1946, p. 1.

23. Fitzpatrick to Truman, August 2, 1946, OF 204-Misc., Truman Papers.

24. *New York Times,* August 6, 1946, p. 6.

25. *Ibid.,* August 1, 1946, p. 10.

26. *Ibid.,* July 28, 1946, p. 29; August 7, 1946, p. 1.

27. Truman, *Memoirs,* 2:152–53.

28. *Forrestal Diaries,* p. 180.

29. Ibn-Saud to Truman, July 8, 1946, OF 204-B, Truman Papers.

30. The *New York Times* also reported that it had been learned Britain was unlikely to make any concessions on the issue of the one hundred thousand Jewish immigrants unless the United States decided to share Britain's military and financial burden in Palestine. *New York Times,* July 6, 1946, p. 1; August 2, 1946, p. 8. Truman dismissed any suggestions of such aid. "Of course," the president wrote to Senator Walter George, "I have no intention of attempting to assume the British responsibility in Palestine." Truman to George, October 17, 1946, OF 204-Misc., Truman Papers.

31. James G. McDonald, *My Mission in Israel* (New York, 1951), p. 11.

32. Truman, *Memoirs,* 2:153.

33. Truman to James G. McDonald, July 31, 1946, OF 204-Misc., Truman Papers.

4: TRUMAN SIDES WITH THE ZIONISTS

1. *New York Times,* September 8, 1946, sec. 4, p. 8; September 11, 1946, p. 8.

2. Truman, *Memoirs,* 2:153.

3. *Forrestal Diaries,* p. 188.

4. Chaim Weizmann to Truman, December 12, 1945, OF 204-Misc., Truman Papers.

5. *New York Times,* October 12, 1946, p. 9; September 30, 1946, p. 18.

6. For example, the Greater New York Zionist Actions Committee, in an open letter published on September 30, 1946, called for the administration's firm support in behalf of (1) allowing one hundred thousand Jews to enter Palestine and (2) assisting in the establishment of a Jewish state in Palestine. On the same day, the *New York Times* reported that the Manhattan Zionist Region passed a resolution at their convention which criticized the Democratic party for failing to carry out its platform pledges. *Ibid.,* September 30, 1946, pp. 8, 18.

7. *Ibid.,* October 25, 1945, p. 1.

8. For example, on October 5–6, 1945, Truman received mail from four congressmen (Herman P. Eberharter, Overton Brooks, Erland H. Hedrick, and Estes Kefauver), each of whom asked the president to insist that Britain open Palestine to Jewish immigration. OF 204-Misc., Truman Papers. Also on October 5, two additional congressmen (Frank R. Havenner and Eugene J. Keogh) notified Truman that they believed it was time for the administration to commit itself to aiding Zionist efforts to establish a homeland for Jews in Palestine. *Ibid.*

9. Alfred Steinberg, "Mr. Truman's Mystery Man," *Saturday Evening Post,* December, 24, 1949, pp. 24, 69–70.

10. Frank Manuel, an historian actively involved in the American Zionist movement during the late 1940s, told the author that

Niles frequently served as a "wailing wall" for minority group leaders as they registered their complaints against the administration. Interview with Frank Manuel, October 26, 1968, New York City.

11. Steinberg, "Mr. Truman's Mystery Man," p. 69. According to Steinberg, one friend of Niles added: "I would say that [in the case of Niles] the passion might be more accurately described as a mania."

12. Sachar, "Niles and United States Policy," p. 3. Much of Sachar's information concerning Niles's unusual working habits came from an interview he had with Jeanette G. Hurley, Niles's White House secretary. Not only did Niles refuse public appearances and dislike big parties, but he was even "wary about transacting affairs on papers. . . ."

13. Steinberg, "Mr. Truman's Mystery Man," p. 24.

14. Niles to William F. Rosenblum, president, Synagogue Council of America, April 5, 1948, OF 204-Misc., Truman Papers.

15. Connelly to Freedman, September 5, 1946, OF 204-Misc., Truman Papers. See also memorandum, Connelly to Niles, September 3, 1946, OF 204-Misc., Truman Papers, in which Connelly asked Niles to prepare a draft of a reply to be sent by Connelly.

16. Epstein to Nahum Goldman, October 9, 1946, Weizmann Archives. Epstein later changed his name to the Hebrew Eliahu Eilat.

17. Sachar, "Niles and United States Policy," pp. 24, 34, 48. A good example of such correspondence appears in the Weisgal-Niles exchange discussed on page 36. Sachar's material is based on the Niles papers at Brandeis University.

18. *Ibid.,* p. 48. The conversation with Lord Inverchapel took place on November 17, 1946.

19. *Ibid.,* p. 41. The author of this telegram is not identified.

20. Weizmann to Niles, February 20, 1949, cited in Sachar, "Niles and United States Policy," p. 2.

21. Memorandum, Weisgal to Niles, April 5, 1946, cited in Sachar, "Niles and United States Policy," pp. 24–25. On April 16, 1946, Niles gave Truman the draft of the proposed message.

On April 18, Truman wrote the following to Niles: "Thanks for
. . . the suggested message. It was sent."

22. Memorandum, Russell to Niles, February 26, 1946, cited in
Sachar, "Niles and United States Policy," p. 23.

23. Memorandum, Niles to Charles G. Ross, June 13, 1946,
cited in *ibid.,* p. 33.

24. Wise to Niles, June 18, 1946, cited in *ibid.,* p. 34. "I am
not prepared," wrote Wise, "to hurt the interests of the American
and British people . . . to spite a man [Bevin] however nasty his
speech and however lamentable his conduct against Zionism."

25. Memorandum, Niles to Truman, May 27, 1946, OF 204-
Misc., Truman Papers. Also see Truman's request for Niles's
views on Palestine. Memorandum, Truman to Niles, May 23,
1946, OF 204-Misc., Truman Papers.

26. Sharett to Niles, March, 1951, cited in Sachar, "Niles and
United States Policy," p. 2.

27. *Forrestal Diaries,* p. 361.

28. When Lessing Rosenwald, president of the anti-Zionist
American Council for Judaism, asked to see the president, Truman's staff agreed to allow an interview, but only after the election. Rosenwald to Truman, October 1, 1946, OF 204-Misc.,
Truman Papers. On the bottom of the letter is written (author unidentified): "OK after Election."

29. From a memorandum written by Roberta Barrows, Matthew J. Connelly's secretary, June 20, 1946, dealing with Niles's
conversation with Truman on the subject of Celler's proposal. OF
204-Misc., Truman Papers. The extent of Niles's evasion is evi-
dent throughout Barrow's memorandum: "Dave Niles talked to the
President about this, and the President is not going to see them.
Dave suggested we wait until Friday and phone Cellers [*sic*], as
Cellers [*sic*] would be out of town by that time, and [a White
House secretary] could leave word with his [Celler's] secretary.
[The White House secretary] can say Mr. Connelly was in New
York and did not return as early as hoped which is why [the
White House is] late in calling." Also see memorandum, author
unidentified, to Connelly, June 19, 1946, OF 204-Misc., Truman
Papers. The message to Connelly informed him that Celler had

phoned "again" about the New York congressional delegation's
wish to meet with Truman. "He [Celler] said he talked to you
[Connelly] and Niles, but neither had given him an answer. He
said that the members of the delegation were becoming impatient
and that Democrats and Republicans alike were apt to give out
statements to the papers that the administration was refusing to
see them on the Palestine question." The writer of the memorandum had just phoned Niles, who had spoken with Celler a few
moments earlier. "Mr. Niles thinks perhaps you had better ask the
President again."

30. Celler to Matthew J. Connelly, June 25, 1946, OF 204-
Misc., Truman Papers.

31. New York Times, July 31, 1946, p. 5. This account of the
session was reported by the *New York Times* and verified by
Celler in an interview with the author on October 29, 1968, in
New York City.

32. This was reported by Eliahu Epstein in a letter to Nahum
Goldman, October 9, 1946, Weizmann Archives.

33. *Ibid.* Epstein makes reference to the Crum/Niles letter to
Hannegan, but does not specify what it says.

34. *Forrestal Diaries,* pp. 346–47. Forrestal's diary entry for
December 3, 1947, reads in part: "He [former Secretary of State
Byrnes] said that Niles and Sam Rosenman [counsel to the president for both Roosevelt and Truman] were chiefly responsible for
the President's decision; that both had told the President that
Dewey was about to come out with a statement favoring the Zionist position on Palestine, and that they had insisted that unless the
President anticipated this movement New York State would be
lost to the Democrats." Byrnes was serving as secretary of state in
1946 when the effort was made to obtain a statement from the
president prior to the election of that year.

35. Memorandum, Clayton to Truman, September 12, 1946,
cited in Sachar, "Niles and United States Policy," p. 42. Apparently a copy of the memorandum wound up with the Niles papers
at Brandeis University.

36. Memorandum, Truman to Clayton, no date, cited in Sachar, "Niles and United States Policy," p. 43.

37. *New York Times,* October 5, 1946, p. 2.

38. *Ibid.,* October 7, 1946, p. 1.

39. Celler to Truman, October 7, 1946, OF 204-Misc., Truman Papers.

40. Robert E. Hannegan, chairman, Democratic National Committee, to Truman, October 17, 1946, OF 204-Misc., Truman Papers.

41. *New York Times,* October 5, 1946, p. 1.

42. Epstein to Goldman, October 9, 1946, Weizmann Archives. The pertinent section reads: ". . . I have renewed my conversations with our friend [Niles] about the [Truman's Yom Kippur] statement. I indicated the increased importance of it in view of the deadlock which has been reached in our unofficial discussions in London."

43. Specifically, certain Jewish leaders did not approve of Truman's call for a "bridging of the gap" between the Jewish Agency's plan for a national home and Grady's proposals. This aspect of the statement was not enlarged on by the press, and the newspapers emphasized Truman's support for a Jewish state. *Ibid.* Typical of the concern displayed was a telegram sent by Epstein to Goldman, October 4, 1946, Weizmann Archives. The text of the telegram read: "Expect serious opposition our circles here [United States] on Government support promised to bridge gap between [Jewish] Agency and British proposals rather than full support our proposal. Spoke [AZEC co-chairman Abba Hillel] Silver who agreed with my suggestion necessity for us concentrate this moment constructive aspects statement."

44. Wise to Niles, October 7, 1946, and October 24, 1946; both cited in Sachar, "Niles and United States Policy," p. 46. Wise's telegram of October 7 read: "I shall probably within the next few days withdraw from the Emergency Council. I certainly will unless the Council is prepared at a special meeting tomorrow to speak in terms of genuine commendation of the President's act."

45. Epstein to Goldman, October 9, 1946, Weizmann Archives.

46. *New York Times,* October 31, 1946, p. 1; November 21, 1946, p. 14.

47. Ibn-Saud to Truman, October 15, 1946, OF 204-Misc., Truman Papers.

48. Truman to ibn-Saud, October 28, 1946, OF 204-Misc., Truman Papers.

49. *New York Times,* November 1, 1946, p. 17.

50. *Forrestal Diaries,* p. 218.

5: BRITAIN GOES TO THE UNITED NATIONS

1. *New York Times,* April 18, 1948, sec. 4, p. 5. Correspondent Dana Adams Schmidt wrote in his analysis of the British policy that Attlee and Bevin were particularly anxious to maintain their military bases in Iraq and Trans-Jordan.

2. *Ibid.,* February 6, 1947, p. 3.

3. *Ibid.,* February 27, 1947, p. 4.

4. *Ibid.,* February 6, 1947, p. 3; February 8, 1947, p. 1; February 9, 1947, p. 1; February 10, 1947, p. 6.

5. Erskine B. Childers, "Palestine: The Broken Triangle," *Modernization of the Arab World,* ed. Jack H. Thompson and Robert D. Reischauer (Princeton, 1966), pp. 156–59.

6. *New York Times,* February 14, 1947, p. 12; February 13, 1947, p. 18.

7. *Ibid.,* February 15, 1947, p. 1.

8. Truman, *Memoirs,* 2:154.

9. Great Britain, *Parliamentary Debates* (Commons), 5th ser., 433 (1947): 1906, 1908.

10. *New York Times,* February 27, 1947, p. 4.

11. *Ibid.* Another Zionist leader, Abba Hillel Silver, chairman of the American Zionist Emergency Council, termed Bevin's statement a "most mischievous distortion." Frank Manuel quotes an unidentified Jewish leader who called Bevin's remarks on a settlement "fantastic nonsense." Manuel, *American-Palestine Relations,* p. 331.

12. Epstein to Goldman, October 9, 1946, Weizmann Archives; *New York Times,* February 27, 1947, p. 4.

13. Truman, *Memoirs,* 2:154.

14. Draft of proposed statement on Bevin's remarks, authored by Secretary of State James Byrnes, February 27, 1947, OF 204-Misc., Truman Papers.

15. *Public Papers of the Presidents of the United States, 1947* (Washington, D.C., 1963), p. 152.

16. *New York Times,* February 26, 1947, p. 1; February 27, 1947, p. 4; February 28, 1947, p. 2.

17. See the "Bevin Folder," OF 204-Misc., Truman Papers; *New York Times,* February 26, 1947, p. 1; February 27, 1947, pp. 1, 4.

18. *New York Times,* April 3, 1947, p. 1; April 14, 1947, p. 1; April 27, 1947, p. 48.

19. United Nations, General Assembly, *Official Records,* First Special Session, "Plenary Meetings of the General Assembly," 68th Plenary Meeting, April 28, 1947, pp. 1–11.

20. Telegram, Stephen Wise to Truman April 30, 1947, OF 204-Misc., Truman Papers; *New York Times,* May 1, 1947, p. 3; May 4, 1947, p. 43. In his telegram, Wise told Truman that he was "pained" to learn of the American stand. In deciding to back the British proposal, Wise wrote, the United States "has taken a position in spirit utterly at variance with the attitude of our Government throughout a whole generation. . . ."

21. United Nations, General Assembly, *Official Records,* First Special Session, "Plenary Meetings of the General Assembly," 75th Plenary Meeting, May 5, 1947, pp. 114–15; 76th Plenary Meeting, May 7, 1947, pp. 116, 122. The Jewish Agency presented its case on May 8, 1947, and the Arab Higher Committee was heard the next day. *Ibid.,* "Main Committee," 50th–52d Meetings (A/C.1/136), May 8–9, 1947, pp. 105–98.

22. *Ibid.,* "Plenary Meetings of the General Assembly," 79th Plenary Meeting, May 15, 1947, pp. 175–77.

23. *Forrestal Diaries,* p. 304; *New York Times,* May 7, 1947, p. 5.

24. Durward V. Sandifer, acting legislative counsel, State Department, to Wagner, June 4, 1947, Wagner Papers.

25. *New York Times,* May 10, 1947, p. 4; June 1, 1947, p. 12; July 4, 1947, p. 4; July 7, 1947, p. 3; July 24, 1947, p. 9.

26. *Ibid.*, January 3, 1946, p. 3.

27. *Ibid.*, February 12, 1946, p. 2.

28. *Ibid.*, April 2, 1948, p. 9.

29. *Ibid.*, March 20, 1947, p. 10; March 31, 1947, p. 4. In addition, the author confirmed these reports in an interview with Clifton Daniel (a witness of conditions at the Cyprus camps in 1947), October 28, 1968, New York City.

30. *New York Times,* July 19, 1947, p. 1.

31. *Ibid.*, August 1, 1947, p. 1.

32. *Public Papers of the Presidents . . . , 1947,* p. 267.

33. *New York Times,* May 20, 1947, p. 1. The protest had also been made earlier in the year. See *ibid.*, January 7, 1947, p. 12.

34. *Ibid.*, June 7, 1947, p. 4. The alleged "illegal acts" the Jews referred to were those British policies which limited Jewish immigration into Palestine.

35. Epstein to Goldman, October 9, 1946, Weizmann Archives.

36. Folder June–August, 1947, Box 773, OF 204-Misc., Truman Papers. Many writers were displeased by Truman's June statement related to the Jewish terrorist organizations. As one letter noted, the president should concern himself with a way to "stop the pogrom of Jews" in Palestine.

37. Telegram, Zionist District of Sussex County, New Jersey, to Truman, September 4, 1947, OF 204-Misc., Truman Papers. An example of a similar type of letter from an individual arrived from a Brooklyn, New York, critic who noted with disgust that she understood that Truman had said he could do nothing for the Jews on the *Exodus.* "Well, there is nothing I can do about seeing you reelected," this writer added. Ruth Preminger to Truman, August 4, 1947, OF 204-Misc., Truman Papers.

38. Joseph Abbell to Truman, August 19, 1947, and memorandum, Truman to Niles, August 23, 1947, cited in Sachar, "Niles and United States Policy," p. 61. This memorandum is among the Niles papers at Brandeis University.

39. Telegram, Wise to Truman, August 1, 1947, and Truman to Wise, August 6, 1947, OF 204-Misc., Truman Papers.

40. Memorandum, Niles to Truman, July 29, 1947, cited in Sachar, "Niles and United States Policy," p. 60. This document is among the Niles papers at Brandeis University.

41. *Ibid.*

42. *New York Times,* September 19, 1947, p. 17.

43. UNSCOP membership included Australia, Canada, Czechoslovakia, Guatemala, India, Iran, Netherlands, Peru, Sweden, Uruguay, and Yugoslavia.

44. United Nations, General Assembly, *Official Records,* Second Session, "United Nations Special Committee on Palestine," Report to the General Assembly, Annex 5 (A/AC.13/NC/16), June 13, 1947, p. 5.

45. *New York Times,* July 23, 1947, p. 7; July 24, 1947, p. 9. The one Arab League member not joining in the uncompromising statement was Trans-Jordan. Making clear her more moderate position, Trans-Jordan invited UNSCOP to hold a separate hearing in Amman.

46. *Ibid.,* June 14, 1947, p. 4.

47. The representatives of the following states supported partition: Canada, Czechoslovakia, Guatemala, Netherlands, Peru, Sweden, and Uruguay. United Nations, General Assembly, *Official Records,* Second Session, "United Nations Special Committee on Palestine," Report to the General Assembly, Recommendations (A/364), September 3, 1947, pp. 42–65.

48. The three nations who signed the minority report were India, Iran, and Yugoslavia. Australia did not endorse either report. *Ibid.,* pp. 8, 59–64.

6: THE UNITED NATIONS APPROVES PARTITION

1. United Nations, General Assembly, *Official Records,* Second Session, "Ad Hoc Committee on the Palestinian Question," Second Meeting, September 26, 1947, pp. 2–4; 15th Meeting, October 16, 1947, pp. 96–98. Britain's decision was met by broad approval at home. The public had tired of an involvement that during the previous year alone had cost 160 million dollars, and had tied down one hundred thousand troops. *New York Times,* November 16, 1947, sec. 4, p. 4.

2. *New York Times,* September 25, 1947, p. 1; September 26, 1947, p. 10; October 9, 1947, p. 1.

3. *Ibid.,* October 10, 1947, p. 1; October 11, 1947, p. 1; October 13, 1947, p. 1.

4. Truman, *Memoirs,* 2:155; *New York Times,* October 12, 1947, p. 1.

5. Safran, *United States and Israel,* pp. 35, 43, 45.

6. *New York Times,* October 12, 1947, p. 1.

7. Speculation in Washington was that Soviet support was based on a desire to have Britain removed from Palestine and possibly gain a foothold in the Middle East by participating in an international police force that might be sent into the Holy Land. *Forrestal Diaries,* p. 410.

8. *New York Times,* March 3, 1947, p. 1.

9. David Horowitz, *State in the Making* (New York, 1953), p. 287.

10. *New York Times,* October 30, 1947, p. 16; November 22, 1947, p. 6.

11. Chaim Weizmann, *Trial and Error: The Autobiography of Chaim Weizmann* (New York, 1949), pp. 457–59. Weizmann recalled the session with Truman with pleasure:

"I was extremely happy to find that the President read the map very quickly and very clearly. He promised me that he would communicate at once with the American delegation at Lake Success.

"At about three o'clock in the afternoon of the same day, Ambassador Herschel Johnson, head of the American delegation, called in Mr. [Moshe] Shertok [head of the Jewish Agency's delegation to the United Nations] . . . in order to advise him of the decision on the Negev, which by all indications excluded Akaba from the Jewish State. Shortly after Mr. Shertok entered, but before the subject was broached, the American delegates were called to the telephone. At the other end of the wire was the President . . . , telling them that he considered the proposal to keep Akaba within the Jewish state a reasonable one, and that they should go forward with it. When Mr. Johnson and . . . [John] Hilldring emerged from the telephone booth after a half-hour conversation, they returned to Mr. Shertok, who was waiting for them, tense with anxiety. All they had for him was the casual remark: 'Oh, Mr. Shertok, we really haven't anything important to tell you.' Obviously the President had been as good as his word, and a few short hours after I had seen him had given the necessary instructions to the American delegation" (*ibid.*, p. 459).

Note that the Moshe Shertok named in the above narrative is the Moshe Sharett mentioned elsewhere in this text. Shertok later changed his name to the Hebrew Sharett.

12. United Nations, General Assembly, *Official Records,* Second Session, "Ad Hoc Committee on the Palestinian Question," 22d Meeting, November 19, 1947, p. 144; 34th Meeting, November 25, 1947, pp. 222–23; Annex 19, pp. 242–69; Annex 25, pp. 270–303.

13. *Ibid.,* "United Nations Special Committee on Palestine," Report to the General Assembly, vol. I (A/364), September 3, 1947, p. 54.

14. Sami Hadawi, *Bitter Harvest: Palestine between 1914–1967* (New York, 1967), p. 14; Fred J. Khouri, *The Arab-Israeli Dilemma* (Syracuse, 1968), p. 7.

15. Khouri, *Arab-Israeli Dilemma,* pp. 7–9; Hadawi, *Bitter Harvest,* p. 14.

16. Khouri, *Arab-Israeli Dilemma,* pp. 11–12.

17. Nejla Izzeddin, *The Arab World: Past, Present, and Future* (Chicago, 1953), pp. 226–27, 249.

18. Khouri, *Arab-Israeli Dilemma,* p. 13.

19. Izzeddin, *Arab World,* pp. 228–29; Harry Howard, *The King-Crane Commission* (Beirut, 1963), pp. 224–26.

20. Khouri, *Arab-Israeli Dilemma,* p. 10; Adler, "Palestine Question in the Wilson Era," p. 327.

21. *New York Times,* March 3, 1947, p. 1.

22. Edward B. Glick, *Latin America and the Palestine Problem* (New York, 1958). Glick persuasively argues the case that the

Jewish Agency organized a superbly thorough campaign to cultivate the votes of Latin American countries. Even before the
United Nations was established, the Jewish Agency made a determination that Latin American support might prove decisive
should the world organization ever handle the Palestine issue.
Years of careful work were rewarded when the twenty Latin
American states responded in the fall of 1947 and cast the following votes: 14 in favor of partition, 1 opposed, and 6 abstentions.

23. Jorge García-Granados, *The Birth of Israel* (New York,
1948), p. 264.

24. *New York Times,* November 26, 1947, p. 4.

25. Horowitz, *State in the Making,* pp. 254, 300.

26. After writing this part of the telegram, Baruch thought better of including it in the final draft. Swope was an ardent supporter of the Zionist cause. The message sent to Swope read: "I
quite understand [*New York Times* publisher Arthur Hays] Sulzberger's position. It has always seemed to me that the whole question never approached except emotionally." Baruch was responding to Swope's telegram of November 27, which read in part:
"Following your telegram talked Sulzberger. He promised editorial calling on abstainers to vote [in the United Nations balloting on partition]. It's not much but it's something because he says
he has no conviction as to issue." Draft of a telegram, Bernard
Baruch to Herbert Bayard Swope, undated; telegram, Swope to
Baruch, November 27, 1947, Baruch Papers, Princeton University, Princeton, N.J.

27. *Congressional Record,* 80th Cong., 1st sess., 1947, p. A5239.

28. Abba Hillel Silver, chairman, American Zionist Emergency
Council, to Wagner, December 11, 1947, Wagner Papers; Trygve
Lie, *In the Cause of Peace* (New York, 1954), p. 162; Glick,
Latin America and the Palestine Problem, pp. 36, 37, 93.

29. Welles, *We Need Not Fail,* p. 63; also see Joseph Dunner,
The Republic of Israel: Its History and Its Promise (New York,
1950), p. 80.

30. Telegram, Celler to Truman, November 26, 1947, OF
204-Misc., Truman Papers.

31. Telegram, Lipsky to Truman, November 28, 1947. For

other messages along the same line, see telegram, Arthur L. Jacobs, general manager, *Jewish Morning Journal,* to Truman, November 27, 1947; telegram, Judge Joseph M. Proskauer, president, American Jewish Committee, to Truman, November 27, 1947. All of the above are located in OF 204-Misc., Truman Papers.

32. Truman, *Memoirs,* 2:158. The president's annoyance was indicated in a letter to Senator Wagner. Truman to Wagner, October 1, 1947, Wagner Papers.

33. *New York Times,* November 28, 1947, p. 1. As far back as October 20 the Zionist leadership had expressed its concern that the United States had not followed up its October 11 endorsement of partition by contacting the United Nations delegations of countries that would usually follow the American lead. Hamilton wrote that United States delegate sources acknowledged that the independent delegations would be left to decide the issue for themselves. Zionist spokesmen were quoted as saying that a two-thirds vote in the General Assembly would be difficult unless the American delegation "goes down the line" in obtaining additional support. *Ibid.,* October 20, 1947, p. 1. Supporters of the Zionist cause charged that officials in the State Department had ordered the American delegation not to use its influence to line up votes for partition. *Ibid.,* November 26, 1947, p. 1.

34. Proskauer to Truman, November 27, 1947 OF 204-Misc., Truman Papers.

35. Horowitz, *State in the Making,* p. 301.

36. Telegram, Celler to Truman, November 26, 1947, OF 204-Misc., Truman Papers. Besides specifically mentioning Greece as a country that should be approached, Celler noted this "same suggestion applies equally to countries such as Haiti, China, Ecuador, Liberia, Honduras, and Paraguay, all of which in the Ad Hoc Committee have abstained or voted adversely."

37. Celler to Truman, December 3, 1947, OF 204-Misc., Truman Papers. There was some movement in favor of the partition plan on the part of the seven countries that Celler specifically urged contacting (see preceding footnote). Two states that abstained during the Ad Hoc Committee vote, Haiti and Liberia, voted in favor of partition in the final balloting. Paraguay, absent

during the committee consideration, cast a favorable vote on November 29. China and Honduras both continued their policy of abstaining through the committee and final vote. Celler had incorrectly included Ecuador on his original list; Ecuador cast ballots in favor of partition on both occasions. Greece moved from an abstaining position to a vote against partition.

38. Celler to Connelly, December 3, 1947, OF 204-Misc., Truman Papers.

39. *Congressional Record,* 80th Cong., 1st sess., 1947, p. 1100.

40. John H. Hilldring is the delegate quoted. Thomas J. Hamilton, "Partition of Palestine," *Foreign Policy Reports,* February 15, 1948, p. 291.

41. García-Granados, *Birth of Israel,* p. 269. Also see *New York Times,* November 28, 1947, p. 1.

42. Glick, *Latin America and the Palestine Problem,* p. 106. The delegate quoted was unidentified.

43. Horowitz, *State in the Making,* pp. 255, 301. Emphasis added.

44. Shapiro to Senator Robert Wagner, December 8, 1947, Wagner Papers.

45. The Boston businessman, Thomas Pappas, sent Niles copies of the cables "that I and a few friends, such as Spyros Skouras (New York Motion Picture Executive) have sent out. . . . The only thing I regret is that you did not speak to me last week when we would have had more time to do something and we could have put on a lot more pressure. With such limited time to do anything, I do not know how successful we can be. As explained to you on the telephone, we did everything humanly possible." The cables, sent to the foreign minister and the prime minister of Greece, appealed on behalf of the suffering Jewish people, and did not mention in any way that Greece was indebted to the United States, and thus should follow the American lead on partition. Pappas to Niles, November 26, 1947, cited in Sachar, "Niles and United States Policy," p. 71. Pappas's letter is among the Niles papers at Brandeis University.

46. García-Granados, *Birth of Israel,* p. 266; *New York Times,* November 27, 1947, p. 1; Glick, *Latin America and the*

Palestine Problem, pp. 107–8. Glick has argued that Cuba, El Salvador, and Honduras were each susceptible to pressure from the American government. Yet Cuba, whose economic fate was tied to the United States, voted against partition. Small and powerless Honduras and El Salvador, two other nations economically dependent upon the United States, both abstained.

47. *New York Times,* November 29, 1947, p. 1.

48. United Nations, General Assembly, *Official Records,* Second Session, "Plenary Meetings of the General Assembly," 128th Meeting, November 29, 1947, pp. 1424–25. The roll-call vote in the General Assembly on November 29 follows:

For partition (33): Australia, Belgium, Bolivia, Brazil, Canada, Costa Rica, Czechoslovakia, Denmark, Dominican Republic, Ecuador, France, Guatemala, Haiti, Iceland, Liberia, Luxembourg, Netherlands, New Zealand, Nicaragua, Norway, Panama, Paraguay, Peru, Philippines, Poland, South Africa, Soviet Union, Sweden, Ukraine, United States, Uruguay, Venezuela, and White Russia.

Against partition (13): Afghanistan, Cuba, Egypt, Greece, India, Iran, Iraq, Lebanon, Pakistan, Saudi Arabia, Syria, Turkey, and Yemen.

Abstentions (10): Argentina, Chile, China, Colombia, El Salvador, Ethiopia, Honduras, Mexico, United Kingdom, and Yugoslavia.

Absent (1): Siam.

For purposes of comparison the Ad Hoc Committee vote of November 25 is also listed (*ibid.,* "Ad Hoc Committee on the Palestine Question," 34th Meeting, November 25, 1947, pp. 222–23):

For partition (25): Australia, Bolivia, Brazil, Canada, Chile, Costa Rica, Czechoslovakia, Denmark, Dominican Republic, Ecuador, Guatemala, Iceland, Nicaragua, Norway, Panama, Peru, Poland, South Africa, Soviet Union, Sweden, Ukraine, United States, Uruguay, Venezuela, and White Russia.

Against partition (13): Afghanistan, Cuba, Egypt, India, Iran, Iraq, Lebanon, Pakistan, Saudi Arabia, Siam, Syria, Turkey, and Yemen.

Abstentions (17): Argentina, Belgium, China, Colombia, El Salvador, Ethiopia, France, Greece, Haiti, Honduras, Liberia,

Luxembourg, Mexico, Netherlands, New Zealand, United Kingdom, and Yugoslavia.

Absent (2): Paraguay and Philippines.

49. *Ibid.,* "Plenary Meetings," pp. 1424–25.

50. Alfred M. Lilienthal, *What Price Israel?* (Chicago, 1953), pp. 63–66; Roosevelt, "Partition of Palestine," pp. 14–15; *Forrestal Diaries,* p. 358; García-Granados, *Birth of Israel,* pp. 266–68. All four accounts purport to give the "inside story" of the scramble for votes, but each source must be read with extreme caution. The first three are written by staunch opponents of the establishment of a Jewish state, and García-Granados was a loyal ally of the Jewish Agency.

51. Jack Redding, *Inside the Democratic Party* (Indianapolis, 1958), p. 146; *Forrestal Diaries,* pp. 309, 345.

52. *Forrestal Diaries,* p. 309.

53. *Ibid.,* p. 323.

54. *Ibid.,* p. 344.

55. Memorandum, Niles to Matthew J. Connelly, October 13, 1947, OF 204-Misc., Truman Papers.

56. For example, New York State Democratic party leaders, including state chairman Paul E. Fitzpatrick and Brooklyn borough president John Cashmore, followed the lead of the powerful New Jersey Democrat Frank Hague and asked Truman to support the partition plan. *New York Times,* October 7, 1947, p. 13. Also see similar statements by Democratic leaders reported in *ibid.,* September 15, 1947, p. 4; and September 18, 1947, p. 14. The following messages received at the White House also urged presidential support for partition: telegram, thirty-five state governors to Truman, October 6, 1947; and Emanuel Celler to Truman, October 13, 1947, OF 204-Misc., Truman Papers.

57. Telegram, Wagner to Truman, September 29, 1947, Wagner Papers.

58. Truman to Wagner, October 1, 1947, Wagner Papers.

7: THE AMERICAN REVERSAL

1. "U.S., U.S.S.R. Support Palestine Partition," *United Nations Weekly Bulletin,* October 21, 1947, p. 532.

2. *Forrestal Diaries,* p. 342; García-Granados, *Birth of Israel,* p. 251.

3. Lie, *Cause of Peace,* p. 163.

4. *Ibid.; New York Times,* December 4, 1947, p. 1; December 9, 1947, p. 16; January 7, 1948, p. 1.

5. Carl Hermann Voss, chairman, Executive Committee, American Christian Palestine Committee, to Robert Wagner, December 5, 1947, Wagner Papers; see also *New York Times,* December 2, 1947, pp. 13, 14; December 3, 1947, p. 5.

6. *Forrestal Diaries,* pp. 346, 376–77, 410–11.

7. Weizmann, *Trial and Error,* p. 471.

8. Maurice Bisgyer, *Challenge and Encounter* (New York, 1967), pp. 190–91.

9. Thirty members of the House of Representatives to Secretary of State George C. Marshall, February 10, 1948, Clark M. Clifford Papers, Truman Library, Independence, Mo. (cited hereafter as Clifford Papers). On March 19, 1948, a group of forty-one congressmen protested against the "lack of vigor and firmness" in regard to American support for partition. *Congressional Record,* 80th Cong., 2d sess., 1948, p. A1664. White House secretaries were inundated with correspondence bearing identical messages, asking the president to work for prompt implementation. For an example, see the collection of 122 cards, letters, and telegrams that Representative John W. Hesselton of Massachusetts forwarded to the White House. Hesselton to Truman, February 14, 1948, OF 204-Misc., Truman Papers.

10. For copies of the newspaper advertisements, see the Democratic National Committee Press Clipping File, Truman Library, Independence, Mo.

11. See Alexander Feinberg's dispatch in the *New York Times,* March 12, 1948, p. 8. On December 2, twenty thousand celebrants attempted to enter a New York City hall that seated only five thousand in order to participate in a rally supporting the United Nations vote on partition. *Ibid.,* December 3, 1947, p. 1.

12. Truman to M. J. Slonim, president, St. Louis Council, American Jewish Congress, March 6, 1948, OF 204-Misc., Truman Papers.

13. Truman, *Memoirs,* 2:160.

14. Matthew J. Connelly, secretary to the president, to Weizmann, February 12, 1948, Weizmann Archives.

15. Memorandum, Jacobson to Dr. Josef Cohn, April 1, 1952, Weizmann Archives. Cohn had written to Jacobson and requested an account of Jacobson's role in the establishment of a Jewish state in Palestine.

16. The telegram is quoted in Bisgyer, *Challenge and Encounter,* pp. 190–91.

17. Memorandum, Jacobson to Cohn, April 1, 1952, Weizmann Archives.

18. *Ibid.*

19. Bisgyer, *Challenge and Encounter,* p. 193.

20. Unsigned memorandum summarizing Somer's telephone message, February 12, 1948, OF 204-Misc., Truman Papers.

21. Moore to Matthew J. Connelly, secretary to Truman, February 9, 1948, OF 204-Misc., Truman Papers.

22. Leon Blank to Truman, February 1, 1948, OF 204-Misc., Truman Papers.

23. *New York Times,* February 18, 1948, p. 1; confirmed in an interview with Moscow on October 28, 1968, in New York City.

24. Robert A. Divine, "The Cold War and the Election of 1948," *Journal of American History* 59 (June 1972): 94.

25. Edgar Eugene Robinson, *They Voted for Roosevelt* (Stanford, 1947), pp. 130, 199.

26. *New York Times,* February 18, 1948, p. 1. In 1946 the Democratic incumbent, Benjamin J. Rabin, defeated the ALP candidate. Complete results in 1946 were: Rabin (Democratic), 39,280 (44 percent); Roy Soden (ALP), 24,373 (27 percent); David Scher (Republican), 17,062 (19 percent); Bernice Benedick (Liberal), 8,167 (9 percent). The 1948 results in the 24th district were: Leo Isacson (ALP), 22,697 (56 percent); Karl Propper (Democratic), 12,578 (31 percent); Dean Alfange (Liberal), 3,840 (9 percent); Joseph De Nigris (Republican), 1,482 (4 percent).

27. *Ibid.*

28. *Ibid.,* February 17, 1948, p. 18; February 11, 1948, p. 23; February 16, 1948, p. 5.

29. *Ibid.,* February 18, 1948, p. 1. The quotation is from Warren Moscow's analysis of the election. Another *New York Times* reporter, Clayton Knowles, wrote that normally Democratic voters swung to Isacson "chiefly on the Palestine issue." *Ibid.,* February 21, 1948, p. 1.

30. *Ibid.,* February 5, 1948, p. 13; February 19, 1948, p. 1.

31. *Ibid.,* February 21, 1948, p. 1. Isacson's election had a sobering effect on the state's Democrats. Within a week, Fitzpatrick, speaking for the Democratic State Committee, publicly endorsed a program calling for a United Nations force that was strikingly similar to what Wallace had called for while campaigning for Isacson. *Ibid.,* February 24, 1948, p. 3.

32. Telegram, Farbman to Truman, February 19, 1948, OF 204-Misc., Truman Papers.

33. *New York Times,* February 7, 1948, p. 1.

34. Lie, *Cause of Peace,* p. 166; *New York Times,* February 17, 1948, p.1.

35. *Forrestal Diaries,* p. 346.

36. *Ibid.,* pp. 374–76, 386, 411. On several other occasions the Joint Chiefs told the president the United States could not afford to send more than a token force to Palestine. Truman, *Memoirs,* 2:162.

37. Arab League sources were reported by the United Press to have said that if American troops were used in Palestine to enforce partition, the United States oil concessions in Saudi Arabia would be ended. *New York Times,* December 11, 1947, p. 23. The Associated Press reported that ibn-Saud was preparing to inform American oil representatives that because of strong public sentiment, he would be compelled to reconsider Saudi Arabia's oil concessions. *Ibid.,* December 22, 1947, p. 12.

38. *Ibid.,* December 19, 1947, p. 1.

39. *Ibid.,* February 22, 1948, p. 1.

40. *Forrestal Diaries,* pp. 356–57.

41. Truman, *Memoirs,* 2:162.

42. *Ibid.* Forrestal to Hanson Baldwin, June 16, 1948, cited in Robert H. Ferrell, *George C. Marshall,* vol. 15 of *The American Secretaries of State and Their Diplomacy,* ed. Samuel F. Bemis

and Robert H. Ferrell, 17 vols. (New York, 1927–67), p. 197; *Forrestal Diaries,* p. 362. One military spokesman in Syria said that if it were necessary, the Arabs would line up with the "devil" (meaning the Soviet Union) if America tried to implement partition with armed force. *New York Times,* January 19, 1948, p. 3.

43. *Forrestal Diaries,* p. 410.

44. *Ibid.,* pp. 347, 359, 365, 376–77. Also see James Reston's article in the *New York Times,* January 27, 1948, p. 8.

45. Forrestal also received a pessimistic response from Democrats James Byrnes and J. Howard McGrath. *Forrestal Diaries,* pp. 347–48, 359–60, 363, 364–65, 372, 376–77.

46. *Ibid.,* pp. 360, 362.

47. *New York Times,* February 13, 1948, p. 16.

48. *Forrestal Diaries,* pp. 371–72.

49. Members of the commission were Bolivia, Czechoslovakia, Denmark, Panama, and the Philippines. United Nations, General Assembly, *Official Records,* Second Special Session, "United Nations Palestine Commission," Report to the General Assembly (A/364), September 9, 1947, pp. 1, 4.

50. *Ibid.,* pp. 4–10. When the commission asked to proceed to Palestine to begin its work, Great Britain said it would not be admitted until two weeks before the mandate terminated on May 15, 1948.

51. *Ibid.,* pp. 10, 12.

52. United Nations, Security Council, *Official Records,* Third Year, 253d Meeting (S/Agenda 253), February 24, 1948, pp. 265–69.

53. *New York Times,* February 25, 1948, p. 1.

54. Truman, *Memoirs,* 2:159.

55. Even before the Czech crisis of early 1948, Truman expressed his concern over having American Troops tied down in Palestine. The president referred to the strategic liabilities during a cabinet meeting on December 1, 1947. *Forrestal Diaries,* p. 346.

56. *Ibid.,* p. 387.

57. Although the memorandum itself is undated, it is filed together with other dated material that Clifford wrote a short time

after the reversal. Memorandum on the reversal of Palestine policy, written by Clifford, undated, Clifford Papers. The text of the memorandum regarding Marshall's March 8 contact with Austin: "Marshall to Austin March 8. President has approved draft statement."

58. Redding, *Inside the Democratic Party,* pp. 148–49.

59. Clark Clifford, undated memorandum on the reversal of Palestine policy, Clifford Papers. Loy Henderson told the writer that the final text Austin used was, with the exception of a few minor word changes, the same one that Truman had approved. From an interview with Henderson, who was in 1948 the director of the State Department's Office of Near Eastern and African Affairs. The interview took place on November 4, 1968, in Washington, D.C.

60. See pp. 77–78 of this chapter.

61. United Nations, Security Council, *Official Records,* Third Year, 271st Meeting (S/Agenda 270), March 19, 1948, pp. 159–68.

62. Pieced together from the Clifford memorandum on the reversal of Palestine policy, Clifford Papers; an interview with Loy Henderson on November 4, 1968; and an interview with Robert McClintock (who at the time of the reversal was the special assistant to the director of the State Department's Office of Special Political Affairs) on November 6, 1968, in Washington, D.C.

63. Jonathan Daniels, *The Man of Independence* (Philadelphia, 1950), p. 318. Another account that removes the responsibility for the reversal from the administration is in Alfred Steinberg, *The Man from Missouri: The Life and Times of Harry S. Truman* (New York, 1962), p. 307. Similarly, in the biography *Harry S. Truman,* Margaret Truman also denies that her father had approved Austin's speech reversing the American position. She cites the following note made by Truman on his calendar: "The State Dept. pulled the rug from under me today. I didn't expect that would happen. . . . The first I know about it is what I see in the papers! Isn't that hell? I am now in the position of a liar and a double-crosser. I've never felt so in my life." Placing the full blame on "insubordination" among State Department personnel, Margaret Truman writes that the episode was "one of the worst

messes of my father's career, and he could do nothing about it but suffer." Margaret Truman, *Harry S. Truman* (New York, 1973), pp. 388–89.

64. Truman, *Memoirs,* 2:163.

8: THE AMERICAN PROPOSAL FOR A UNITED NATIONS TRUSTEESHIP

1. United Nations, Security Council, *Official Records,* Third Year, 271st Meeting (S/Agenda 270), March 19, 1948, pp. 167–68.

2. *New York Times,* March 20, 1948, p. 1.

3. United Nations, Security Council, *Official Records,* Third Year, 271st Meeting, March 19, 1948, p. 167.

4. The request for a truce was added to the American plan on March 30, 1948. *Ibid.,* 275th Meeting (S/Agenda 275), March 30, 1948, p. 247; *New York Times,* March 21, 1948, sec. 4, p. 4; March 30, 1948, p. 15.

5. Secretary-General Trygve Lie has written that "Washington took the heart out of any support which the Security Council might have mobilized to enforce peace and maintain the decision on partition." Lie, *Cause of Peace,* pp. 167–68.

6. The quotation is taken from the text of a memorandum by Clark Clifford concerning a White House conference on Palestine. The following persons were present: Truman, Marshall, Henderson, Rusk, McGrath, Connelly, Niles, Counselor of the State Department Charles E. "Chip" Bohlen, Federal Security Administrator Oscar Ewing, Presidential Press Secretary Charles G. Ross, and Clifford.

7. Sharett to Marshall, April 29, 1948, OF 204-Misc., Truman Papers. One week later Sharett again clearly rejected the State Department plan for a truce in another letter to Marshall. Sharett to Marshall, May 7, 1948, OF 204-Misc., Truman Papers.

8. *New York Times,* May 14, 1948, p. 1.

9. *Ibid.,* March 26, 1948, p. 12.

10. Sharett to Marshall, May 7, 1948, OF 204-Misc., Truman Papers.

11. *New York Times,* March 26, 1948, p. 11.

12. United Nations, Security Council, *Official Records,* Third Year, 277th Meeting (S/Agenda 277), April 1, 1948, pp. 33–35.

13. *New York Times,* April 9, 1948, p. 1.

14. *Ibid.,* May 4, 1948, p. 1.

15. Lie, *Cause of Peace,* p. 170.

16. *New York Times,* May 5, 1948, p. 1; May 7, 1948, p. 8.

17. Clifford spoke with Dean Rusk, director of the State Department's Office of Special Political Affairs, on May 8, 1948. Rusk said the number one United States priority was to arrange a truce before May 15, but if an armistice were not obtained, a simplified trusteeship for Palestine could still be approved by the General Assembly. Memorandum of a conversation between Clifford and Rusk, May 8, 1948, written by Clifford on the same day, Clifford Papers.

18. See Thomas J. Hamilton's dispatch on this subject, *New York Times,* May 4, 1948, p. 1.

19. *Ibid.,* May 6, 1948, p. 1; Lie, *Cause of Peace,* p. 172.

20. García-Granados, *Birth of Israel,* p. 278; Lie, *Cause of Peace,* p. 172.

21. *New York Times,* May 13, 1948, p. 1.

22. Dr. Erique Rodríguez, Uruguay's representative at the United Nations, was one of many delegates who believed that the United Nations had made its decision in November, 1947, and that the integrity of the world organization depended upon implementation. Bitterly asking the assembled delegates, "What are we here for?" he was gavelled down on the opening day of the special session. *New York Times,* April 17, 1948, p. 1.

23. *New York Times* writer Thomas Hamilton pointed out that some critics saw "an obvious parallel between the United Nations' current predicament and the crisis that plagued the old League of Nations in the Ethiopian case. In both instances the collective will of the civilized world was thwarted by armed force—Italy invaded Ethiopia, and the Arabs have shown the determination to resist the partition plan." *Ibid.,* April 18, 1948, sec. 4, p. 5.

24. The day after Austin's speech on March 19, 1948, Lie conferred with the American ambassador and expressed his "sense of

shock and of almost personal grievance." Stating that the new United States policy was "a rebuff to the United Nations and to me," Lie recommended that Austin join him in resigning "as a measure of protest against [Austin's] instructions." Lie was eventually persuaded that resigning would serve no good purpose. Lie, *Cause of Peace,* pp. 170–71.

25. According to the commission's report, the armed hostility of Arabs, both inside and outside Palestine, "the lack of co-operation from . . . [Britain], the disintegrating security situation in Palestine, and the fact that the Security Council did not furnish the Commission with the necessary armed assistance, are the factors which made it impossible for the Commission to implement the Assembly's [partition] resolution." United Nations, General Assembly, *Official Records,* Second Special Session, "United Nations Palestine Commission Report to the General Assembly" (A/532), April 10, 1948, pp. 36, 39.

26. Lie wrote that once it was clear the United States was not intent on implementing partition, "firm action by the Security Council or its permanent members was out of the question." Lie, *Cause of Peace,* p. 169.

27. Irwin Ross, *The Loneliest Campaign* (New York, 1968), p. 20; Patrick Anderson, *The President's Men: White House Assistants of Franklin D. Roosevelt, Harry S Truman, Dwight D. Eisenhower, John F. Kennedy and Lyndon B. Johnson* (New York, 1968), pp. 88, 113–15. Ross has written a thoroughly engaging account of President Truman's upset victory in the 1948 election. Anderson's volume, which examines the roles played by the key presidential aides since the 1930s, provides an insight into the operation of Truman's White House staff.

28. Anderson, *President's Men,* pp. 90, 113, 116–17; Ross, *Loneliest Campaign,* p. 20.

29. Memorandum, "The Politics of 1948," Clifford to Truman, November 19, 1947, Clifford Papers.

30. Ross, *Loneliest Campaign,* pp. 26–27, 273; Divine, "Cold War and the Election of 1948," p. 93.

31. Memorandum, "The Politics of 1948," Clifford to Truman, November 19, 1947, Clifford Papers.

32. *Ibid.*

33. See pp. 83–86 above.

34. The four men recommended to Truman that the arms embargo be lifted "as soon as possible." The advice was given during a White House conference on the Palestine issue, March 24, 1948. Memorandum of a Conference on Palestine, March 24, 1948, written by Clifford on April 24, 1948, Clifford Papers.

35. Statement by the president, March 25, 1948, OF 204-Misc., Truman Papers. Various drafts of the statement are available in the Clifford Papers. In one draft Clifford suggested that Truman's statement emphasize the president's continuing support for a Jewish homeland, and explain that the trusteeship was to be temporary, pending the time when the Jewish national home could be established. The following language was recommended by Clifford: "Palestine as a Jewish National Home is a fundamental principle of American foreign policy. This belief is a very profound personal conviction with me, one which I devoutly hope may successfully come to fruition very soon." Draft of a Presidential Statement on Palestine, written by Clifford, spring, 1948, Clifford Papers. Clifford's recommendation was not accepted.

36. See pp. 89–90 and 93–94 above.

37. *New York Times,* March 21, 1948, sec. 4, p. 8.

38. *Ibid.,* March 24, 1948, p. 1; April 2, 1948, p. 9.

39. *Ibid.,* March 21, 1948, p. 6.

40. *Ibid.,* March 20, 1948, p. 3. New York Republican Congressman Jay LeFevre wrote to the president: "Many of my constituents daily are protesting to me the decision of our Government to withdraw its support" for partition. LeFevre asked Truman to "stop this floundering around." Representative LeFevre to Truman, April 1, 1948, OF 204-Misc., Truman Papers. The 50th Assembly District Democratic Council in California was one of many party organizations to censure the president: "We strongly disapprove your present vacillating policy." Telegram, Democratic Council, 50th Assembly District, California, to Truman, March 27, 1948, OF 204-Misc., Truman Papers.

41. Memorandum, Knutson to Nash, June 24, 1951, Nash Files. Much of the mail was of a highly emotional nature. For example: "Oh, how could you stoop so low! . . . You act for the colonial interests of England, gangster Arabs, and oil. . . . Won't

you stop trying to be a statesman and act like a human being!"
Samuel and Katherine Sloan to Truman, March 19, 1948, OF
204-Misc., Truman Papers.

42. During March, April, and early May, the White House received many form letters urging a pro-Jewish Palestine policy.
They are included among the president's papers. OF 204-Misc.,
Truman Papers. What little public support Truman did receive for
the reversal was of dubious value. The president of the American
Council for Judaism, an anti-Zionist organization that had little
influence within the Jewish community, informed Truman that his
group "subscribes wholeheartedly to the new American plan."
Telegram, Lessing Rosenwald to Truman, March 22, 1948, OF
204-Misc., Truman Papers.

43. Max Lowenthal to Clifford, March 26, 1948; telegram,
Bartley Crum to Clifford, April 21, 1948, Clifford Papers. Both
Lowenthal, an influential New York lawyer, and Crum were
staunch supporters of the Zionist cause.

44. Redding, *Inside the Democratic Party,* p. 166.

45. *Ibid.,* p. 148; *New York Times,* March 23, 1948, p. 1.

46. *New York Times,* April 17, 1948, p. 9.

47. Telegram, Dr. Isaac Levine, New York State committee-
man (19th Assembly District, Brooklyn), and Assemblyman
Philip J. Schuhler, delegate to the National Convention, to Truman, March 23, 1948, OF 204-Misc., Truman Papers.

48. *New York Times,* March 22, 1948, p. 26.

49. *Ibid.,* April 5, 1948, p. 1; April 15, 1948, p. 7.

50. Harry H. Vaughan, military aide to the president, had
asked Truman to receive representatives of a group that favored
reversal. On the bottom of the request, someone in the White
House (author unidentified) had noted that the group had been advised "that the President was seeing no groups on the Zionist subject." Memorandum, Vaughan to Truman, March 31, 1948, OF
204-Misc., Truman Papers.

51. Weizmann's letter commented, "The choice for our people,
Mr. President, is between Statehood and extermination." The let-
ter was filed with the following notation: "Not ans'd. RAC [Rose
A. Conway, administrative assistant in the president's office.]"

Weizmann to Truman, April 9, 1948, OF 204-Misc., Truman Papers.

52. Truman to Congressman Bloom, April 23, 1948, OF 204-Misc., Truman Papers.

53. *New York Times,* April 29, 1948, p. 16.

9: AMERICAN RECOGNITION OF ISRAEL

1. The increasing military activity can be traced in the following dispatches: *New York Times,* March 28, 1948, p. 1; May 2, 1948, p. 1; May 14, 1948, p. 5.

2. Sharett to Marshall, April 29, 1948, Clifford Papers.

3. Sharett to Marshall, May 7, 1948, Clifford Papers. It was suggested to Sharett that Arab, Jewish, and American representatives be flown to Palestine immediately, in an airplane furnished by the president, to seek a truce. On May 4, Sharett told Dean Rusk that this "somewhat spectacular proceeding now suggested" was unwarranted. Telegram, Sharett to Rusk, May 4, 1948, Clifford Papers.

4. Memorandum of a conversation between Clifford and Rusk on May 8, 1948, written by Clifford, May 8, 1948, Clifford Papers. When Clifford mentioned that there was a strong indication of actual partition, along the lines of the United Nations resolution, already existing in Palestine, Rusk denied that this was the case. Rusk claimed the Jews controlled only about one-third of the area allotted to the proposed Jewish state. When full-scale civil war erupted on May 15, military intelligence proved that Rusk had seriously underestimated the extent of Jewish control.

5. See p. 93 above.

6. Memorandum, "The Politics of 1948," Clifford to Truman, November 19, 1947, Clifford Papers.

7. Rosenman to Clifford, May 9, 1948, Clifford Papers.

8. Memoranda, Lowenthal to Clifford, May 7, 1948 (two); May 8, 1948; May 9, 1948; May 11, 1948; May 12, 1948 (two), Clifford Papers.

9. Chaim Weizmann to Truman, May 13, 1948; Frank Goldman, president, B'nai B'rith, to Truman, May 14, 1948; telegram,

Senator Robert Wagner, honorary chairman, and Dean Alfange, chairman, Committee to Arm the Jewish State, to Truman, May 8, 1948; Rabbi Samuel Thurman to Truman, May 13, 1948. All the above are located in OF 204-Misc., Truman Papers.

10. Weizmann to Truman, May 13, 1948, OF 204-Misc., Truman Papers.

11. Sol Bloom, *The Autobiography of Sol Bloom* (New York, 1948), p. 297. In a telegram sent the day following his conference with the president, Bloom urged Truman to allow the United States to become the first nation to recognize the new state on May 15. Telegram, Bloom to Truman, May 13, 1948, OF 204-Misc., Truman Papers. Herbert Lehman, a former New York governor and an influential Jewish leader, asked Truman to recognize the Jewish state "as promptly as possible." Lehman to Truman, May 13, 1948, Herbert Lehman Papers, Columbia University, New York, N.Y. New York City Democratic leader Edward J. Flynn also recommended to Truman that the Jewish state be recognized as soon as it came into being. Flynn to Matthew J. Connelly, May 13, 1948, OF 204-Misc., Truman Papers.

12. Truman to Joseph F. Guffey, May 12, 1948; and Albert M. Greenfield to Guffey, May 6, 1948, OF 204-Misc., Truman Papers. Truman was also urged to extend recognition even before the Jewish state was scheduled to come into existence. Telegram, Philip J. Schuhler, member, New York State Assembly, to Truman, May 9, 1948, OF 204-Misc., Truman Papers. Congressional supporters of the Zionists made clear their intention to back the request for immediate recognition of the Jewish state. Petition, thirty-six members of the House of Representatives to Truman, May 7, 1948, OF 204-Misc., Truman Papers. Claiming to represent the wishes of twenty members of Congress who had endorsed their statement, three United States senators—New Hampshire's Charles W. Tobey, Oregon's Wayne Morse, and New Mexico's Dennis Chavez—announced on May 13 that they favored the "prompt recognition of the government of the existing Jewish State." *New York Times,* May 14, 1948, p. 3.

13. Arvey to Truman, May 12, 1948, OF 204-Misc., Truman Papers.

14. *New York Times,* May 2, 1948, p. 64.

15. Memorandum, Niles to Clifford, May 6, 1948, cited in Sachar, "Niles and United States Policy," pp. 89–90. This draft was located by Sachar among the Niles papers at Brandeis University.

16. *New York Times,* May 11, 1948, p. 19; May 12, 1948, p. 16; May 13, 1948, p. 7.

17. From author's interview on November 6, 1968, with Robert McClintock, in 1948 the special assistant to the director of the State Department's Office of Special Political Affairs and one of the men present at the conference on May 12, 1948.

18. *Ibid.*

19. *Ibid.*

20. *Ibid.*

21. Interview with Loy Henderson, undersecretary of state for Near Eastern and African Affairs in 1948; interview with Carlton Savage, a member of the State Department's Policy Planning Staff in 1948. Both interviews took place in Washington, D.C., on November 4, 1968.

22. Clifford later recalled in an interview with Jonathan Daniels, "He said it all in a righteous God-damned Baptist tone." The incident is recounted in Daniels, *Man of Independence,* p. 319.

23. McClintock told the author the president made absolutely no indication regarding "which way he was leaning" as the meeting adjourned. Interview with McClintock, November 6, 1968.

24. Memorandum of Legal Opinions on the Recognition of the Palestine State, prepared by Ernest A. Gross, State Department legal adviser, May 13, 1948, Clifford Papers. According to the memorandum, the recognition policy of the department was based on three factors: "a) *de facto* control of the territory and the administrative machinery of State, including the maintenance of public order; b) the ability and willingness of a government to discharge its international obligations; c) general acquiescence of the people of a country in the government in power." Gross's opinions were attached to a memorandum that Clifford received from C. H. Humelsine, Office of the Secretary of State, May 14, 1948, Clifford Papers. Humelsine wrote: "Mr. Lovett asked that this be sent over for your information."

25. Telegram, Eliahu Epstein, agent, Provisional Government of Israel, to Moshe Sharett, foreign minister, Provisional govern-

ment of Israel, May 14, 1948, Weizmann Archives. In the Clifford Papers there is an undated memorandum, written in Clifford's own hand, concerning his telephone conversation with Epstein.

26. A change was made in the wording of the American statement of recognition, from "the Government of Israel" to "the provisional Government of Israel." Draft of an Announcement of American Recognition, May 14, 1948, OF 204-Misc., Truman Papers. A de facto government is one that is actually functioning, whereas a de jure government is one that is deemed lawful.

27. Telegram, Epstein to Sharett, May 14, 1948, Weizmann Archives.

28. Epstein to Truman, May 14, 1948, OF 204-Misc., Truman Papers. Epstein's telegram to Sharett of the same day clearly shows that regardless of the claim to the contrary in the letter requesting American recognition, Epstein had not been authorized by the designated officials of the new state to tender the message: "Surrounding circumstances are as follows: Clark Clifford White House spokesman telephoned Washington friends [of the Jewish Agency] advising that State Department at noon fourteen May agree immediate recognition in event prompt request therefore received. . . . Wide consultation and prior notification precluded by pledge of secrecy demanded by Clifford. . . . Earlier during day Henderson telephoned to ascertain boundaries of new state. [I] advised that boundaries in accord UN Resolution. . . . Circumstances required that I take title for this act [and] assume responsibility for sending letter." Telegram, Epstein to Sharett, May 14, 1948, Weizmann Archives.

29. Interview with Henderson, November 4, 1968; telegram, Epstein to Sharett, May 14, 1948, Weizmann Archives.

30. Interview with McClintock, November 6, 1968.

31. Cited in Sachar, "Niles and United States Policy," p. 93, based on the Niles papers at Brandeis University.

32. *New York Times,* May 15, 1948, pp. 1, 2. David Ben-Gurion, who became the state's first prime minister, read the following proclamation: "We hereby proclaim the establishment of the Jewish state in Palestine, to be called Israel."

33. White House Press Release, May 14, 1948, OF 204-Misc., Truman Papers.

34. *New York Times,* May 15, 1948, pp. 1, 3.

35. From a dispatch by *New York Times* correspondent George Barrett. *Ibid.,* May 15, 1948, p. 3.

36. The delegate who asked for a verification was Dr. Albert González Fernandez of Colombia. United Nations, General Assembly, *Official Records,* Second Special Session, "Plenary Meetings of the General Assembly," 141st Plenary Meeting, May 14, 1948, pp. 36–37.

37. New York Times, May 15, 1948, p. 1. Because the press learned of the story before the United States delegation received any information, "the mortification of the American representatives," as Secretary-General Lie later recalled, "was acute." Lie, *Cause of Peace,* p. 173.

38. United Nations, General Assembly, *Official Records,* Second Special Session, "Plenary Meetings of the General Assembly," 141st Plenary Meeting, May 14, 1948, p. 42.

39. *New York Times,* May 15, 1948, p. 3.

40. United Nations, General Assembly, *Official Records,* Second Special Session, "Plenary Meetings of the General Assembly," 141st Plenary Meeting, May 14, 1948, pp. 44–45, 47.

41. Truman was quoted by Niles in a conversation Niles had with Abram L. Sachar in May of 1948; the content of this conversation was confirmed by Truman in a letter to Abram Sachar, March 10, 1959. Cited in Sachar, "Niles and United States Policy," p. 1.

42. It is interesting to note that this point, attributing Truman's motive to a desire to beat the Soviet Union before she could recognize the Jewish state, was never even brought up as a reason for immediate recognition during the conference on May 12, 1948. From an interview with Robert McClintock, November 6, 1948.

43. The total adds up to more than 100 percent because some editorials assigned more than one motive to the president's action.

44. *New York Times,* May 17, 1948, p. 5; telegram, Ben-Gurion to Truman, May 16, 1948, OF 204-Misc., Truman Papers.

Edward Jacobson cabled: "Thanks and God bless you." Telegram, Jacobson to Truman, May 14, 1948, OF 204-Misc., Truman Papers. Also see the complimentary messages to Truman from Herbert Lehman, A. J. Granoff, the officers of the American Jewish Committee, Frank Goldman (president, B'nai B'rith), Emanuel Neumann (president, Zionist Organization of America), OF 204-Misc., Truman Papers.

45. Robert Wagner to Truman, May 17, 1948, Wagner Papers; telegram, Frank W. Buxton to Truman, May 15, 1948, OF 204-Misc., Truman Papers. Congressmen who supported the Zionist cause applauded the president. New York Times, May 15, 1948, p. 3; May 16, 1948, p. 1; May 17, 1948, p. 3. New York City's Mayor William O'Dwyer reportedly told the president that recognition would have a favorable political effect in New York. Ibid., May 16, 1948, p. 4.

46. Bernard H. Sandler to Frank S. Land, May 18, 1948, OF 204-D, Truman Papers.

47. Another seventy-five thousand were turned away after capacity had been reached. New York Times, May 17, 1948, pp. 1, 3.

10: A PRO-ZIONIST MOOD IN WASHINGTON

1. The quotation was reported by the Associated Press to have been taken from an official Jordanian communiqué from Amman. New York Times, May 15, 1948, p. 1.

2. Lie, Cause of Peace, pp. 176, 178–79.

3. United Nations, Security Council, Official Records, Third Year, 302d Meeting, May 22, 1948, p. 59; New York Times, May 27, 1948, p. 3.

4. Khouri, Arab-Israeli Dilemma, pp. 74–81.

5. Lie, Cause of Peace, pp. 185, 187.

6. New York Times, July 9, 1948, p. 1.

7. Ibid., June 9, 1948, p. 1; Lie, Cause of Peace, p. 188.

8. Weizmann is quoted here. During his meeting with the American president, which lasted half an hour, Weizmann asked for a loan of ninety million dollars in order to arm his nation and

to bring fifteen thousand Jewish refugees into Israel each month. Following the conference the Israeli president was optimistic: "My plea for a loan was not in vain." *New York Times,* May 26, 1948, p. 1; Weizmann, *Trial and Error,* pp. 480–81.

9. James G. McDonald, *My Mission in Israel, 1948–1951* (New York, 1951), pp. 4–7; *Forrestal Diaries,* p. 441; *New York Times,* June 23, 1948, p. 24.

10. *Forrestal Diaries,* p. 441.

11. McDonald, *Mission in Israel,* p. 8.

12. Cable, Chaim Weizmann to Truman, June 24, 1948, OF 204-D, Truman Papers. The president of the Zionist Organization of America, Emanuel Neumann, wired Truman to express his organization's gratification over the appointment of McDonald. Telegram, Neumann to Truman, June 24, 1948, OF 204-Misc., Truman Papers.

13. *New York Times,* July 15, 1948, p. 8.

14. *Ibid.,* p. 4.

15. *Ibid.,* February 21, 1948, p. 1. For an account of the February congressional election, see pp. 78–81 above.

16. Memorandum, "The Politics of 1948," Clifford to Truman, November 19, 1947, Clifford Papers.

17. Israeli President Chaim Weizmann, in a letter to Truman on September 6, 1948, asked the American president to grant de jure recognition to the Jewish state. Weizmann to Truman, OF 204-D, Truman Papers. Both of the following messages also urged Truman to extend de jure recognition: M. J. Slonim, president, St. Louis Council, American Jewish Congress, to Truman, September 14, 1948, OF 204-Misc.; petition, 377 Jewish war veterans to Truman, July 26, 1948, OF 204-Misc., Truman Papers.

18. Jacobson to Weizmann, August 6, 1948, Weizmann Archives.

19. Weizmann to Truman, September 6, 1948, OF 204-D, Truman Papers. The American president wrote in reply: ". . . I am glad that Eddie Jacobson informed you of the situation with which we are forced [to deal] and the effort we are putting forth into getting things ironed out." Truman to Weizmann, September 10, 1948, OF 204-D, Truman Papers.

20. E. J. Seigel to Truman, June 10, 1948, General File (Israel), Truman Library, Independence, Mo. Both of the following messages also urged Truman to end the embargo: telegram, Marshall Field and Richard J. Finnegan to Truman, July 9, 1948; and telegram, Fred Caruso, chairman, Democratic party, Cannonsburg, Pa., to Truman, July 11, 1948, OF 204-D, Truman Papers.

21. Memorandum, Charles E. Bohlen, counselor of the State Department, to Clifford, April 18, 1948, Clifford Papers; *Public Papers of the Presidents of the United States, 1948* (Washington, D.C., 1964), p. 279.

22. According to a National Opinion Research Center poll of July 1, 1948, 82 percent of the sampling said they hoped to see the embargo continued, and 8 percent were undecided about changing the policy. Only 10 percent urged that the embargo be lifted. *Public Opinion Quarterly* 12 (Fall, 1948): 550.

23. Eliahu Epstein, special representative of the State of Israel to the United States, to Clifford, August 3, 1948, Clifford Papers; telegram, Bartley C. Crum to Clifford, September 8, 1948, Clifford Papers; memoranda from Max Lowenthal to Clifford on the following dates: May 17, 1948 (two); May 20, 1948; May 29, 1948 (two); May 30, 1948; May 31, 1948; June 1, 1948; and June 17, 1948, Clifford Papers; Clifford to M. J. Slonim, president, St. Louis Council of the American Jewish Congress, June 23, 1948, Clifford Papers.

24. Clifford to Slonim, June 23, 1948, Clifford Papers. Shortly after full recognition was granted to Israel in 1949, Clifford wrote to Eliahu Epstein. Clifford noted that de jure recognition "was a realization of a hope which you and I and other stalwarts had had for some time. I know that it brought to you as it did to me, a real sense of fulfillment." Clifford to Epstein, February 8, 1949, Clifford Papers.

25. Bowles to Clifford, September 23, 1948, Clifford Papers.

26. William R. Schafer, chairman, Democratic Committee, Sullivan County, New York, and Cecile R. Pockross, chairman, Youth Division of Sullivan County Democrats, to Truman, October 12, 1948, OF 204-Misc., Truman Papers. Also see similar advice from Alfred A. Lama, member, New York State Assembly, to Truman, July 8, 1948, OF 204-Misc., Truman Papers.

27. Fred G. Moritt, member, New York State Senate, to Truman, June 16, 1948, OF 204-D, Truman Papers. Also see Edward F. Seiller, Democratic campaign chairman, Louisville, Ky., to William M. Boyle, Jr., assistant national chairman, Democratic National Committee, September 23, 1948, OF 204-D, Truman Papers. Seiller suggested that the president announce on Yom Kippur that he was granting de jure recognition and economic aid to Israel.

28. Alan Smith to Truman, May 29, 1948, OF 204-D, Truman Papers.

29. M. D. Swartz to Truman, June 29, 1948, OF 204-D, Truman Papers. The correspondence on Israel indicates that most of the Jews were pleased with the president's attitude toward Israel. As one writer told Truman, a number of his friends had formed a speaker's bureau "to awaken American Jewry to the fact that you are the redeemer of Israel. Be strong because God of Abraham, Isaac, and Jacob is with you." Benjamin N. Goldberg to Truman, July 8, 1948, OF 204-Misc., Truman Papers. There was a feeling among some Jews, however, that Truman had not done enough. For example: "More SWEET WORDS are just meaningless—they are CHEAP! We want ACTION to help Israel. You are playing dumb to Israel's pleas! The voters will also turn deaf ears to your pleas for votes in November—tit for tat!" Zion Actions Committee of New York to Truman, July 23, 1948, OF 204-Misc., Truman Papers.

11: TRUMAN'S PRE-ELECTION APPEAL TO AMERICAN JEWRY

1. *New York Times,* September 18, 1948, p. 1.

2. Sharett sent the following message to Secretary-General Lie: "Outraged by abominable assassination . . . by desperadoes and outlaws who are execrated by entire people of Israel and Jewish community of Jerusalem." Lie, *Cause of Peace,* p. 190.

3. *New York Times,* September 21, 1948, p. 1.

4. From an interview with McClintock on November 6, 1968.

5. "Statement by Secretary Marshall," *Department of State Bulletin,* October 3, 1948, p. 436.

6. *New York Times,* July 15, 1948, p. 8.

7. *Ibid.,* September 23, 1948, p. 5; September 26, 1948, p. 10; September 29, 1948, p. 1; October 4, 1948, p. 1.

8. Cable, Weizmann to Jacobson, September 27, 1948, OF 204-D, Truman Papers. Jacobson forwarded Weizmann's cable to the president's secretary, Matthew J. Connelly, "hoping that it will convince the boss how urgent it is for him to act immediately." Jacobson to Connelly, September 30, 1948, OF 204-D, Truman Papers.

9. Cable, Robert A. Lovett, undersecretary of state, to Clifford, September 21, 1948, Clifford Papers.

10. A memorandum on the unfavorable political response to Marshall's acceptance was received by William M. Boyle, Jr., a political troubleshooter for the president who was aboard the presidential campaign train. Boyle later became chairman of the Democratic National Committee. Memorandum, Max Siskind to Boyle, September 23, 1948, Clifford Papers.

11. Telegram, Crum to Clifford, September 28, 1948, Clifford Papers.

12. Cable, Lovett to Clifford, undated, Clifford Papers.

13. Lovett cabled the following message to Clifford: "Believe the sentence suggested [in Clifford's previous cable] will meet the problem. I understand it now reads, 'It seems to me that the Bernadotte plan offers a basis for continuing efforts to secure settlement.'" Cable, Lovett to Clifford, undated, Clifford Papers. The proposed presidential statement also included an assurance of de jure recognition "promptly" following the election of a permanent Israeli government. Draft, proposed statement by the president, written by Clifford, undated, Clifford Papers.

14. Truman, *Memoirs,* 2:167.

15. Draft, proposed memorandum, Truman to Marshall, written by Clifford, September 29, 1948, Clifford Papers.

16. Truman, *Memoirs,* 2:167.

17. Governor Dewey, who frequently claimed that he had introduced the principle of bipartisanship in foreign policy during the 1944 campaign, insisted he would continue to support the present administration's foreign policy in 1948. "The nations of the

world can rest assured," Dewey pledged, "that the American people are in fact united in their foreign policy." Ross, *Loneliest Campaign,* pp. 168, 207, 214, 218–19, 266.

18. Memorandum, Boyle to Matthew J. Connelly, October 13, 1948, OF 204-D, Truman Papers. Boyle also noted: "That doesn't mean that others cannot speak out on the question or that the President should not receive a committee. But it should be a committee promising President Truman their support and in appreciation of his past record and present stand rather than a committee asking for more promises out of him."

19. The statement was drafted by Clifford. Memorandum, Truman to Marshall, October 17, 1948, Clifford Papers.

20. Memorandum regarding a telephone message from C. T. Anderson of Railway Labor's Political League, J. B. C. Howe to Clifford, October 5, 1948, Clifford Papers. Also see telegram, 14th Assembly District Democratic Club, New York, to Truman, October 28, 1948, OF 204-D, Truman Papers.

21. In a three-quarter-page newspaper advertisement, the American Zionist Emergency Council demanded that Truman clarify the administration's position. *New York Times,* October 20, 1948, p. 33.

22. Cable, Charles S. Murphy to Clifford, September 30, 1948, Clifford Papers; *New York Times,* October 1, 1948, p. 1; October 12, 1948, p. 7.

23. *New York Times,* October 23, 1948, p. 7. Joseph B. Keenan, who headed the American Federation of Labor's League for Political Education, carefully noted in a message sent to the president's campaign entourage that the *New York Herald Tribune* had emphasized that "Governor Dewey in effect repudiated the Truman Administration's Palestine policy yesterday." According to Keenan, "Dewey and his aides are definitely making a political issue preparatory to his final drive in New York State." Keenan to Matthew J. Connelly, October 23, 1948, Clifford Papers.

24. Memorandum, Clifford to Truman, October 23, 1948, Clifford Papers.

25. Statement by the president, October 24, 1948, OF 204-Misc., Truman Papers.

26. *Ibid.; New York Times,* October 29, 1948, p. 1.

27. *New York Times,* October 29, 1948, p. 6.

28. *Ibid.,* October 31, 1948, p. 65.

12: THE JEWISH VOTE AND THE AFTERMATH OF THE ELECTION

1. Lawrence Fuchs's study indicates that Wallace won from 12 to 27 percent of the vote in heavily Jewish wards. Lawrence Fuchs, *The Political Behavior of American Jews* (Glencoe, Ill., 1956), p. 79. Samuel Lubell compiled some data that indicate that many Jews did support Wallace in New York State. Lubell suggests that the Jews, who normally voted Democratic, switched to Wallace in many instances because of Truman's vacillation on the Palestine–Israel issue. He offers no statistical evidence, however, to back up this view. Samuel Lubell, "Who Really Elected Truman," *Saturday Evening Post,* January 22, 1949, p. 56.

2. The same study estimated that Wallace received between 15 and 20 percent of the national Jewish vote in 1948. Herbert H. Hyman and Paul B. Sheatsley, "The Political Appeal of President Eisenhower," *Public Opinion Quarterly* 17 (Winter, 1953): 443–61. A public opinion study of the predominantly Jewish 50th ward in Chicago indicates that Truman received 96.2 percent of the votes cast for the Republican and Democratic candidates. Although the study does not take into account the vote for Wallace, it does suggest that Truman was able to stop a mass defection to Dewey. Maurice G. Guysenir, "Jewish Vote in Chicago," *Jewish Social Studies* 20 (October 1958): 200.

3. Daniel J. Elazar, "American Political Theory and the Political Notions of American Jews: Convergences and Contradictions," in Peter J. Rose, ed., *The Ghetto and Beyond* (New York, 1969), p. 216.

4. Svend Petersen, *A Statistical History of the American Presidential Elections* (New York, 1963), pp. 102–3; *American Jewish Yearbook,* vol. 52, *1951* (New York, 1951), pp. 17–21.

5. White House Press Release, January 19, 1949, Clifford Papers. In a letter of appreciation, President Chaim Weizmann told Truman the people of Israel "are deeply aware of how much we

owe you personally for this most helpful decision." Weizmann to Truman, June 2, 1949, OF 204-D, Truman Papers.

6. White House Press Release, January 31, 1949, OF 204-D, Truman Papers. De jure recognition was followed by the elevation of James G. McDonald, who had served as special representative of the United States to Israel since June 22, 1948, to the rank of ambassador. "United States and Israel Exchange Ambassadors," *Department of State Bulletin,* March 6, 1949, p. 302.

7. See p. 130 above.

8. Alfred Steinberg's sympathetic account of Truman's tenure in the White House quoted David Niles as saying that "tears were running down Truman's cheeks" following the rabbi's remark. Steinberg, *Man from Missouri,* p. 308.

9. Memorandum, Jacobson to Dr. Josef Cohn, April 1, 1952, Weizmann Archives.

10. Telegram, Marc Siegel, publicity director, Mizrachi Women's Organization, to Truman, November 19, 1948, OF 204-D, Truman Papers. An example of how readily Truman not only accepted, but encouraged, the belief that he had been a consistent sponsor of Zionist programs can be seen in the president's address to the Mobilization Conference of the National Jewish Welfare Board on October 17, 1952. Recalling with precision his effort to open Palestine to one hundred thousand refugees, Truman completely omitted mention of his reversal of policy early in 1948. "You know the rest of the story as well as I do," the president declared. "The Jewish Agency for Palestine went ahead with plans to partition Palestine and proclaim the state of Israel. I am proud of my part in the creation of this new state. Our Government was the first to recognize the state of Israel. Dr. Chaim Weizmann is an old and dear friend of mine. It was a great pleasure for me to have him stay overnight in the Blair House. I could not help but notice the many thousands of people who passed by the Blair House to see the flags of the United States and the new country of Israel flying side by side." "Mr. Truman's Message to Jewish Welfare Board," *U.S. News and World Report,* October 31, 1952, pp. 82–84.

11. Lie, *Cause of Peace,* p. 191; Walter Eytan, *The First Ten Years: A Diplomatic History of Israel* (New York, 1958), p. 29.

12. "Armistice between Egypt and Israel," *Department of State Bulletin,* March 6, 1949, p. 302; Khouri, *Arab–Israeli Dilemma,* pp. 95–98; Theodore Draper, *Israel and World Politics: Roots of the Third Arab–Israeli War* (New York, 1968), p. 10; Lie, *Cause of Peace,* pp. 191–92; Eytan, *First Ten Years,* pp. 29–33, 41, 43–44. Since no viable Arab state had been created in Palestine, as proposed by the partition resolution, Jordan and Egypt enlarged their territory; Jordan annexed one portion of Palestine and the Egyptians occupied another part. Draper, *Israel and World Politics,* p. 10.

Selected and Annotated Bibliography

MANUSCRIPT COLLECTIONS

Independence, Mo. Harry S. Truman Library. Clark M. Clifford Papers. An extremely valuable collection for this study, Clifford's papers contain a wealth of candid material on the behind-the-scenes maneuvering to induce the president to adopt a pro-Zionist stance.

————. ————. Philleo Nash Files. These files contain extensive White House surveys relating to the Palestine-Israel public opinion mail.

————. ————. Harry S. Truman Papers. Although the president's Official File for Palestine–Israel does contain an impressive amount of material, it does not include some papers that cast an unfavorable light on Truman's Palestine–Israel policy.

————. ————. Weizmann Archives. The Truman Library has acquired copies of documents relevant to Truman's Palestine–Israel policy from the Weizmann Archives in Rehovoth, Israel. This collection contains information concerning the strategy employed by the Zionists to persuade Truman to adopt pro-Zionist policies.

New York City. New York Public Library. Sol Bloom Papers.

Princeton, N.J. Princeton University. Bernard Baruch Papers.

Washington, D.C. Georgetown University. Robert Wagner Papers.

INTERVIEWS

Emanuel Celler. October 29, 1968. New York, N.Y.

Clifton Daniel. October 28, 1968. New York, N.Y.

Loy Henderson. November 4, 1968. Washington, D.C.

193

Robert McClintock. November 6, 1968. Washington, D.C.
Frank Manuel. October 26, 1968. New York, N.Y.
Warren Moscow. October 28, 1968. New York, N.Y.
Carlton Savage. November 4, 1968. Washington, D.C.

GOVERNMENT DOCUMENTS

A. United States Documents

Congressional Record. 76th to 80th Congress. Washington, D.C., 1939–48.
Public Papers of the Presidents of the United States: Harry S. Truman, 1945–1948. Washington, D.C., 1961–64.

B. Foreign Documents

Great Britain. *Parliamentary Debates* (Commons), 5th ser., 433 (1947).
United Nations. General Assembly. *Official Records,* First Special Session, 1947.
———. ———. *Official Records,* Second Session, 1947.
———. ———. *Official Records,* Second Special Session, 1948.
———. ———. *Official Records,* Third Session, 1948.
United Nations. Security Council. *Official Records,* Third Year, 1948.

MONOGRAPHS AND SPECIAL STUDIES

Glick, Edward B. *Latin America and the Palestine Problem.* New York, 1958. A detailed account of how the Zionists carefully worked for support of their program throughout Latin America.
Sachar, David B. "David K. Niles and United States Policy toward Palestine." Unpublished undergraduate honors thesis, Harvard University, 1959. This is an extraordinarily valuable source since Sachar had access to Niles's papers, a privilege that has not been granted to other researchers.

DIARIES, REMINISCENCES, AND AUTOBIOGRAPHIES

Acheson, Dean. *Present at the Creation: My Years in the State Department*. New York, 1969.

Crum, Bartley C. *Behind the Silken Curtain: A Personal Account of Anglo-American Diplomacy in Palestine and the Middle East*. New York, 1947.

García-Granados, Jorge. *The Birth of Israel: The Drama As I Saw It*. New York, 1949.

Millis, Walter, ed. *The Forrestal Diaries*. New York, 1951. The diaries provide a candid account of Forrestal's struggle to persuade the president to adopt anti-Zionist policies.

Truman, Harry S. *Memoirs*. 2 vols. Garden City, N.Y., 1955–56. Frequently what Truman omits is of more interest than what he discusses. Truman simply evades an examination of the Palestine–Israel decisions that were determined on the basis of political expediency. It is apparent that in writing the *Memoirs,* Truman was eager to show not only that his Palestine–Israel policy was consistent, but that politics played no role in his decisions.

Truman, Margaret. *Harry S. Truman*. New York, 1973.

Weizmann, Chaim. *Trial and Error: The Autobiography of Chaim Weizmann*. New York, 1949.

NEWSPAPERS

New York Herald Tribune. 1945–49.

New York Times. 1945–49.

Washington Post. 1945–49.

(The editorials of eighty-five representative newspapers in the Library of Congress were consulted for reactions to Truman's recognition of Israel on May 14, 1948.)

GENERAL WORKS

Anderson, Patrick. *The President's Men: The White House Assistants of Franklin D. Roosevelt, Harry S. Truman, Dwight*

D. Eisenhower, John F. Kennedy and Lyndon B. Johnson. New York, 1968.

Bailey, Thomas A. *A Diplomatic History of the American People*. 8th ed. New York, 1969.

————. *The Man in the Street: The Impact of American Public Opinion on Foreign Policy*. New York, 1948.

Campbell, John C. *Defense of the Middle East*. New York, 1960.

Daniels, Jonathan. *The Man of Independence*. Philadelphia, 1950.

Feis, Herbert. *The Birth of Israel*. New York, 1969.

Gerson, Louis L. *The Hyphenate in Recent American Politics and Diplomacy*. Lawrence, Kans., 1964.

Halperin, Samuel. *The Political World of American Zionism*. Detroit, 1961.

Horowitz, David. *State in the Making*. New York, 1953. Written by an influential member of the Jewish Agency, this account reveals the extent of the Zionist campaign to win United Nations approval for the partition resolution.

Khouri, Fred J. *The Arab-Israeli Dilemma*. Syracuse, N.Y., 1968.

Lie, Trygve. *In the Cause of Peace*. New York, 1954. Secretary-General Lie places much of the blame on the United States for blocking United Nations efforts to carry out the partition resolution.

Redding, Jack. *Inside the Democratic Party*. Indianapolis, 1958.

Ross, Irwin. *The Loneliest Campaign*. New York, 1968.

Safran, Nadav. *The United States and Israel*. Cambridge, Mass., 1963.

Schechtman, Joseph B. *The United States and the Jewish State Movement: The Crucial Decade, 1939–1949*. New York, 1966.

Slater, Leonard. *The Pledge*. New York, 1970.

Steinberg, Alfred. *The Man from Missouri: The Life and Times of Harry S. Truman*. New York, 1962.

Stevens, Richard P. *American Zionism and U.S. Foreign Policy, 1942–1947*. New York, 1962.

Stein, Leonard. *The Balfour Declaration*. New York, 1961.

Taylor, Alan R. *Prelude to Israel: An Analysis of Zionist Diplomacy, 1897–1947*. New York, 1959.

Index